Sacred Numerical Codes Channeled By Agesta

Om Tsé

Sacred Numerical Codes Channeled By Agesta
Copyright ©2022-
Om Tsé Academy
www.omtse.com
 ISBN: 9798835175260
Independently published

Index

Introduction

The Sacred Numerical Codes are new resources that come to our time with the purpose of accelerating our process of healing, evolution and ascension; Channeled by the teacher José Gabriel Agesta, they are presented as a simple and powerful tool that helps to heal diseases, establish communication with the Divine, repel and or annul low vibration entities and facilitate the planetary ascension process.

The Divinity speaks to us through the numbers, and the Codes are given to us to activate them in a simple and practical way. This is a Manual that can save you multiple incarnations, ease your karma, and comfort your Soul.

The Codes must be repeated in batches of 45 times; 45 is the number of the manifestation and they are activated through faith. You can recite the Code however you feel best; for example the Sacred Code: 1111 all together, (one thousand one hundred eleven) o You can do the number repeating in two digits 11 11 (eleven eleven) o You can do it one by one repeating it by number 1 1 1 1 (one one one one) Use it however you want, the one that suits you and is easier for you. When the codes are separated by commas, or Slash /, Example 29, 2129, 1577 or 29/2129/1577, they are different numbers for the same purpose, and you choose the one with which you vibrate the most.

IMPORTANT: There are no rules, there are no rules, you do not have to say decrees, prayers or mantras to do them, use them wherever you want, anywhere.

where you feel is best for you, no matter what time you do it; You can recite the Code mentally or using your voice. If you get used to the vibration of these numbers, you will tune into Higher Dimensions and develop psychic faculties such as telepathy, clairvoyance, clairaudience and intuition. You can keep the beads counting on your fingers, however I recommend using a necklace or a rope with 45 balls. If you wish, the Om Tsé Academy team can manufacture your personalized necklace made of quartz and stainless steel, for more information write to wasap + (57) 314-2954725 or visit the website: www.omtse.com and leave a message.

Note: When carrying out the cleaning or protection work, sometimes headaches, dizziness, picores, seizures may occur (each person manifests it differently), drink a lot of water that will clean you, for a lifetime we have been accumulating negativity, and it is time to let go.

Blessings in your process,

With love,

Om Tsé

Numerical sacred code activation applied by Om Tsé

Although the teacher Agesta affirms that codes can be activated through the intention that each person has, due to my metaphysical training I use the following method, if you want to adapt it to your life, I present below the way in which I do it:

-According to the will of God, in the name of Jesus Christ, under Grace, in a perfect way and in harmony for the whole world, I ask permission to activate the sacred code number_____ for the purpose of_____.

–Thank you Father and Divine Mother for activating this sacred code in my life.

Note: - After doing the activation round of 45 repetitions, I affirm the word 5 times:

-Activated!

For those who are beginning or beginning with the path of the Agesta Sacred Codes, the CLEANING OF 9 DAYS is the first step.

Why does it seem like the codes are not working? They do work, but we have so much density acquired during this and other lives that it is like peeling an onion. This exercise will go a long way in removing those layers so that abundance, relationship, and other codes work more quickly. Emotional, Psychic, Genetic, Genealogical, Psychological Programming, Limiting beliefs, etc. are balanced.

Keep in mind that this cleansing may involve getting rid of old ways of being based on ego, fear, etc. If you are not willing to be the best version of yourself, "don't do it."

The exercise is done for NINE DAYS ... AND ALL THE CODES IN THIS LISTING ARE ACTIVATED. For 45 times each. EVERY DAY.

KARMIC, EMOTIONAL, PSYCHIC, GENE-ALOGIC AND BELIEF CLEANING CHAN-NELED BY THE AGESTA MASTER, DO ITFOR 9 DAYS - REPEAT EACH CODE 45 TIMES

- With the power of the Golden Cross of Oasibeth, Mother Mary and the Ascended Master Merlin, I now undo all the work that the asyntrions (beings of darkness) have done on me, my loved ones and my benefactors. I seal my aura with the Sacred Code: 19-9-1913, coming from the Divine Light of Planet Ageon and I am now free by Divine order, and forever.

- Violet Flame of the thousand suns, I ask that you transmute any blockage in my life with the Sacred Code 860907.

- Holy Spirit, Sacred Code 443355 for the liberation of many karmic ties and oppressors that have made my life difficult during several incarnations including the current one.

- Sacred Code 442. This Code brings to the surface repressed material from other lives.

- 613 Acángel Miguel (Protection against the forces of evil. Every time you feel fear or fear, for any reason or feel vulnerable, call me and instantly I will protect you mentally, physically and emotionally, I will give you courage, feeding your strength interior and motivation to be more noble and selfless 75139 Clear paths.

- Cancel implants or vibratory barriers "failures" ... Sacred Codes 575, 26, 104 and 1679.

- "Message from the Magician Merlin, channeled by José Gabriel Agesta: There is a type of "implant" that can only be canceled by means of the Sacred Codes that have been given to them. I am referring to a vibrational barrier that I would call "failure", so to speak and adjusting to your language.

- Many of those who will read this channel feel disappointed, sad, and bewildered, because they are stagnant and unable to shake off their visible and invisible oppressors. Despite their valiant efforts, there is something that does not allow them to be free, although they feel the comfort and the beneficent breeze of their Angels and Guides.

- That is why I have come Adored Souls, to put an end to this infamy. This word (implants) seems a bit strong, but it is adequate. Many of you have been mistreated by other entities, and have suffered because of them for many incarnations.

- By means of the Sacred Codes they will make up the time lost in those prisons, and they will get rid of these entities, here in this life. I repeat: Here in this life. Many have not been able to fulfill their missions for the cited cause, so that the Numbers will turn them into urgent shortcuts and they will see miracles. If you use my Sacred Codes and those of My Divine Love Complement, you will feel our presence.

- Inc. Faced with a difficult problem, they will see us ap-pear in their minds with the precise and timely solu- tion. "

- Listen to the me of the past, Sacred Code 000.

- Karmic Contracts (Liberation), Sacred Code 14710.

- Cleaning Astral Larvae 1118. Family Tree (to heal it), Sacred Code 553.

- Eliminate negative factors of genetic inheritance, Sacred Code 314.

- Heal painful memories during the 9 months of permanence in the Maternal Womb, Sacred Code 52.

- Heal overwhelming memories from 9 Months to 7 years of age, Code Sa-degree 919.

- Heal negative memories from 7 to 18 years of age, Sacred Code 59.

- To erase negative memories from the subconscious, Sacred Code 45600.

- Archangel Raphael for healing 29 Heal and act effectively and powerfully in all your bodies. Root out captive aftermath from past and present "black mag-ic" attacks, AngelessHealers Sacred Code 44.

- To free ourselves and cut telepathic ties that bind us to other people, Sacred Code 577.

- To reconcile with the Inner Child, Sacred Code 89.

- Arcangel Chamuel, Sacred Code 725 to heal and / or forgive unbalanced past and present relationships.

- Negative cleanings, Sacred Code 0927, to clean negative spaces, vibrations, objects, people, and entities of all kinds.

- To remove interference from the lower astral, Sacred Code 237.

- To unlock my inner voice, Sacred Code 563.

- Cleanse the aura, Sacred Code 26700.
- Sacred Code to multiply the "signs" 62413.

- Divine Mercy, Sacred Code 7 and 2033.

- Extend Divine Mercy, Sacred Code 18.

- Higher Self, Sacred Code 864.

- Faith, Sacred Code 32 and 414.

- Freedom from the spirit of ruin and misery 773.

- Open roads 691.

- Opening up to new opportunities 1111.

- Job that makes us happy 454545.

- Financial problems (surrender to God) 608.

- Secrets and hidden things, quickly manifest what dreams of. Sacred Code 2020

- King Solomon asking for wisdom and help in cases that seem impossible 344.

- Saint Charbel (You have lived many lives. The painful experiences of the past have made your faith deteriorate. If you come back to me, I will help you to trust yourself, your Angels and Teachers, and God. . Do not allow anyone to intimidate you with the energy of fear. Whoever is trying to scare you is a manipulative being that only seeks to feed on your vital energy. Do not give it your power no matter how threatening it is presented to you. Sacred Code 799.

- Protection of Saint George 118.

THANK YOU 3333

Human Body

Body parts

- **Assimilate strength (muscle development)** … Sacred Code 58154

- **Good health…**Sacred Code 60

- **Physical body….**Sacred Code 512

- **Elemental of the body …**Sacred Code 97

- **Strengthen muscles …**Sacred Code 2710

- **Restore DNA ..**Sacred Code 81621

- **Health and vitality of the physical body …**Sacred Code 900

- **Year…**Sacred Code 927

- **Arms…**Sacred Code Left: 11 / Right: 39

- **Bronchi …**Sacred Code 329

- **Hips …**Sacred Code 711

- **Heart…**Sacred Code 123

- **Left Elbow** ...Sacred Code 7124

- **Right elbow**...Sacred Code 7123

- **Spine**...Sacred Code 304

- **Neck**...Sacred Code 91

- **Teeth**...Sacred Code 15000

- **Gums** ...Sacred Code 681

- **Esophagus**...Sacred Code 52189

- **Ganglia** ...Sacred Code 37600

- **Throat**...Sacred Code 52088

- **Thymus gland** ...Sacred Code 59981

- **Pineal gland**...Sacred Code 52011

- **Pituitary gland**...Sacred Code 11115

- **Internal secretion glands** ...Sacred Code 534

- **Liver**...Sacred Code 76Página **17** de **2132**

- **Right shoulder...**Sacred Code 2769

- **Left shoulder...**Sacred Code 6420

- **Tongue...**Sacred Code 1111

- **Mamas (breasts) ...**Sacred Code 857

- **Left hand...**Sacred Code 555

- **Right hand...**Sacred Code 777

- **Matrix...**Sacred Code 2114

- **Spinal cord...**Sacred Code 79199

- **Myelin ...**Sacred Code 20

- **Virile Member (penis) ...**Sacred Code 333

- **Nose...**Sacred Code 71

- **Eyes...**Sacred Code 385

- **Ears ...**Right: 79 - Left: 74

- **Ovaries ...**Sacred Code 1579

- **Pancreas**...Sacred Code 159

- **Eyelids** ...Sacred Code 114

- **Right foot**...Sacred Code 94

- **Left foot**...Sacred Code 93

- **Legs**...Sacred Code 62070

- **Prostate**...Sacred Code 37

- **Right lung**...Sacred Code 81

- **Left lung**...Sacred Code 15

- **Kidneys**...Sacred Code 37

- **Left kidney**...Sacred Code 105

- **Right kidney**...Sacred Code 106

- **Left knee**...Sacred Code 54

- **Right knee**...Sacred Code 63

- **Circulatory system**...Sacred Code 163

- **Digestive system...**Sacred Code 1520

- **Endocrine system...**Sacred Code 112

- **Immune system...**Sacred Code 616 and 765

- **Lymphatic system...**Sacred Code 2190

- **Muscular system...**Sacred Code 1515

- **Nervous system...**Sacred Code 820

- **Osseous system...**Sacred Code 88 and 513

- **Reproductive system...**Sacred Code 333
- **Respiratory system...**Sacred Code 513

- **Urinary system...**Sacred Code 56

- **Testicles ...**Sacred Code Left 404. Right 408

- **Thyroid...**Sacred Code 67

- **Ankle...**Sacred Code 504

- **Bladder...**Sacred Code 2073

- **Lumbar vertebrae** ...Sacred Code 62731

- **Cervical vertebrae**...Sacred Code 2799

- **Vulva**...Sacred Code 555

Diseases

Eyes and vision

- **Amblyopia...**Sacred Code 3894

- **Astigmatism...**Sacred Code 028 and 14243

- **Optic Nerve Atrophy ...**Sacred Code 1611

- **Bags under the eyes ...**Sacred Code 2190

- **Waterfalls...**Sacred Code 33129

- **Conjunctivitis...**Sacred Code 82115

- **Coloboma in iris ...**Sacred Code 3851

- **Wet macular degeneration ...**Sacred code 386

- **Dry macular degeneration ...**Sacred Code 385

- **Retinal detachment...** Sacred Code 620

- **Eye spill ...** Sacred Code 420

- **Retinal dystrophy ...** Sacred Code 7113

- **Diplopia ...** Sacred Code 61318

- **Visual pain ...** Sacred Code 44415

- **Coats disease ...** Sacred Code 52060

- **Squint...** Sacred Code 52190
- **Exoforia ...**Sacred Code 386

- **Photophobia...**Sacred Code 1190

- **Glaucoma...**Sacred Code 991

- **Neovascular Glaucoma ...**Sacred Code 80120

- **Farsightedness...**Sacred Code 825

- **Maculopathy ...**Sacred Code 380

- **Myopia...**Sacred Code 315

- Optic Neuromyelitis... Sacred Code 389

- **Eye Burns ...**Sacred Code 25914

- **Diabetic retinopathy...**Sacred Code 15700

- **Retinitis Pigmentosa ...**Sacred Code 16500

- **Terigión (fleshy eyes)...** Sacred Code 82109

- **Uveitis ...**Sacred Code 6050

Autoimmune diseases

- **Chronic disease...**Sacred Code 763

- **Asthma...**Sacred Code 2539

- **Arthritis...**Sacred Code 551

- **Osteoarthritis ...**Sacred Code 621

- **Ulcerative colitis...**Sacred Code 18

- **Eczema...**Sacred Code 294

- **Diabetes...**Sacred Code 22574

- **Scleroderma ...**Sacred Code 27600

- **Lateral sclerosis ...**Sacred Code 2114 or 771

- **Ankylosing Spondylitis ...**Sacred Code 1511

- **Fibromyalgia ...**Sacred Code 871

- **Lupus...**Sacred Code 599

- **Myasthenia ...**Sacred Code 1129

- **Myasthenia gravis...**Sacred Code 2113

- **Purpura Autoimmune Trobocytopenia ...**Sacred Code 615

- **Sjogren's syndrome...**Sacred Code 52179

- **Rheumatism...**Sacred Code 2777

- **Vitiligo ...**Sacred Code 515

People of the Third Age

- **Uric acid (Lower)...**Sacred Code 2050

- **Anguish or Panic Disorder (Crisis)...**Sacred Code 1113

- **Anxiety...**Sacred Code 363

- **Alzheimer's (prevent disease)...**Sacred Code 5947

  - **Alzheimer's (people who suffer from it)...** Sacred Code 42913

- **Arthritis...**Sacred Code 551

- **Osteoarthritis ...**Sacred Code 621

- **Kidney Stones ...**Sacred Code 25809

- **Waterfalls...**Sacred Code 33129

- **Sciatica...**Sacred Code 52037

- **Cirrhosis...**Sacred Code 88818

- **Stroke...**Sacred Code 87813

- **Diabetes...**Sacred Code 22574

- **Embolisms ...**Sacred Code 621

- **Mental diseases...**Sacred Code 8977

- **Epilepsy...**Sacred Code 753

- **Schizophrenia...**Sacred Code 2913

- **Pulmonary fibrosis...**Sacred Code 2511
- **Gout...**Sacred Code 120

- **Herniated discs...**Sacred Code 52130

- **Hemorrhoids...**Sacred Code 2579

- **Hepatitis...**Sacred Code 82976

- **Mushrooms...**Sacred Code 2679

- **Urinary infections...**Sacred Code 3334

- **Heart Failure ...**Sacred Code 670

- **Leukemia**...Sacred Code 583

- **Spots on the skin**...Sacred Code 879

- **Memory (lost)**...Sacred Code 574

- **Migraines**...Sacred Code 67918

- **Nerves**...Sacred Code 827

- **Pneumonia**...Sacred Code 1775

- **Degenerative Osteoarthrosis**...Sacred Code 11834

- **Osteopenia**...Sacred Code 11125

- **Parkinson**...Sacred Code 57159

- **Paraplegia**...Sacred Code 881

- **Athlete's foot**...Sacred Code 67987

- **High pressure**...Sacred Code 54721

- **Low pressure**...Sacred Code 11561

- **Circulatory Problems ...**Sacred Code 52311
- **Gastric reflux...**Sacred Code 26700

- **Regenerate cartilage in joints ...**Sacred Code 2929

- **Diabetic retinopathy...**Sacred Code 15700

- **Retinitis pigmentosa ...**Sacred Code 16500

- **Bipolar disorder...**Sacred Code 721

- **Tuberculosis...**Sacred Code 29701

- **Deafness...**Sacred Code 721

- **Warts ...**Sacred Code 31921

- **Vesicle (problems) ...**Sacred Code 801000

- **Vomiting ...**Sacred Code 112

- **Swollen Body Areas ...**Sacred Code 578

Kids

- **Increasing the height of children** ...Sacred Code 52611

- **Type 2 spinal muscular atrophy** ...Sacred code 31560

- **Bulling** ...Sacred Code 52031

- **Stimulate psychomotor skills in Children** ... Sacred Code 2080

- **Phonetics in children (Problems of)** ...Sacred Code 1529

  - **Screaming and angry outbursts in children** ...Sacred Code 1380

- **Interest in studies** ...Sacred Code 220

- **Children with Licencephaly** ...Sacred Code 1689

- **Young children (who do not speak)** ...Sacred Code 1579

- **Autism...**Sacred Code 6927

- **Child care deficit ...**Sacred Code 52557

- **Child brain paralysis...**Sacred Code 71228

Sexuality, Pregnancy and its conditions

- **Increased libido ...**Sacred Code 11834

- **Cancel sexual karma ...**Sacred Code 2516

- **Cut sexual ties with ex-partners ...**Sacred Code 5772

- **Heal negative thoughts about sexuality** ...Sacred Code 3337. For millennia you have been taught that sex is "dirty and bad" and this I repeat, on a subconscious level it has created unhappy lives and discomfort in you. Sexuality is something Divine and I can help you to work on it if you allow me, Erimihala.

- **Sexuality (these codes can be used as General Medicine) ...**Sacred Code 111, 222, 434 and 739

Woman

- **Deviations of the uterus** ...Sacred Code 811

- **Vaginal Tightening** ...Sacred Code 332

- **Dysmenorrhea** ...Sacred Code 191

- **Dyspareunia (painful intercourse)** ...Sacred Code 808

- **Primary Dysfunction** ...Sacred Code 5714 Covers the woman who has never experienced an orgasm.

  - **Secondary dysfunction (loss of orgasmic capacity)** ...Sacred Code 579

- **Menstrual pain**...Sacred Code 82550

  - **Pain and swelling in the walls of the bladder**...Code 28700

- **Sexually transmitted disease** ...Sacred Code 8916

- **Fibroma...**Sacred Code 62711
- **Hypogonadism ...**Sacred Code 25799 and 12611

- **Menopause...**Sacred Code 525

- **Fibroids in the uterus...**Sacred Code 03518

- **Fallopian tube obstruction ...**Sacred Code 2115

- **Ovaries (pain)...**Sacred Code 729

- **Polyps (uterine) ...**Sacred Code 58519
- **Polycystic ovarian disease ...**Sacred Code 1614

- **Ovarian cysts ...**Sacred Code 29800

- **Regulation of estrogen levels ...**Sacred Code 352

- **Regulation of Progesterone levels...**Sacred Code 351

- **Polycystic ovary syndrome...**Sacred code 2915

- **Vaginismus...**Sacred Code 679

Man

- **Cryptorchidism (Undescended Testicle) ...** Sacred Code 2979

- **Primary dysfunction (people who have never had an erection) ...**Sacred Code 3724

- **Secondary dysfunction (Loss of erectile capacity) ...**Sacred Code 8879

- **Orgasmic dysfunction (difficulty ejaculating) ...**Sacred Code 1524

- **Sexually transmitted disease ...**Sacred Code 8916

- **Premature ejaculation ...**Sacred Code 673

- **Sexual performance (Fear of)...**Sacred Code 680

- **Hydrocele...**Sacred Code 474

- **Regulation of testosterone levels...** Sacred Code 350

Pregnancy

- **Increase in the amount of milk in women who are breastfeeding...**Sacred Code 25700

- **Unborn baby...**Sacred Code 912

- **Pregnancy (Achieve or get pregnant)...**Sacred Code 660

- **Pregnancy (Solve problems that arise)...**Sacred Code 52569

- **Infertility...**Sacred Code 660

- **Women about to give birth who suffer anxi-ety, fear, or pain...**Sacred Code 617

- **Cesarean section recovery...**Sacred Code 579

Addictions and states of mind

- **Food Addiction ...**Sacred Code 72469

- **Control addiction...**Sacred Code 271

- **Alcoholism...**Sacred Code 71566

- **Anguish or Panic Disorder (Crisis)...**Sacred code 1113

- **Anxious...**Sacred Code 363

- **Anorexy...**Sacred Code 27600

- **Excessive appetite...**Sacred Code 551

- **Self boycott...**Sacred Code 593

- **Self esteem...**Sacred Code 877

- **Bulimia...**Sacred Code 615

- **Codependency...**Sacred Code 554

- **Nail biting...**Sacred Code 67120

- **Nervous breakdown...**Sacred Code 994

- **Psychotic Crisis ...**Sacred Code 2090

- **Guilt (get rid of) ...**Sacred Code 339

- **Give up smoking...**Sacred Code 811

- **Depression...**Sacred Code 9

- **Drug addiction...**Sacred Code 122714

- **Eliminate the effect of nicotine in the body ...** Sacred Code 1613

- **Balance...**Sacred Code 897

- **Mental diseases...**Sacred Code 8977

- **Stress...**Sacred Code 52579

- **Schizophrenia...**Sacred Code 2913

- **Lack of appetite...**Sacred Code 316

- **Phobias...**Sacred Code 66 or 32

- **Smoking (to quit smoking)...**Sacred Code 25543

- **Unsafety**...Sacred Code 420

- **Insomnia**...Sacred Code 531

- **Gambling** ...Sacred Code 272

- **Mamitis** ...Sacred Code 101

- **Hobbies** ...Sacred Code 1119

- **Afraid**...Sacred Code 680

- **Fear of death (Get rid of)** ...Sacred Code 928

- **Irrational fears** ...Sacred Code 681

- **Misogyny**...Code 891

- **Mythomania** ...Sacred Code 1190

- **Abandonment Neurosis** ...Sacred Code 427

- **Paranoia**...Sacred Code 1559

- **To heal those who suffered sexual abuse intheir childhood** ...Sacred Code 378

- **For people who care excessively ...**Sacred Code 215633. This Number has been revealed to me by the beautiful Ascended Master Kwan Yin. It is used for those addicted to worrying excessively about everything, which notably reduces their quality of life.

- **Hypochondriacal people ...**Sacred Code 26300

- **Perfectionist people ...**Sacred Code 2710

- **Nightmares...**Sacred Code 57721

- **Procrastination ...**Sacred Code 7039

- **Rage...**Sacred Code 201

- **Mental retardation...**Sacred Code 524

- **Parental Alienation Syndrome ...**Sacred Code 62637

- **Desperate situations ...**Sacred Code 19

- **Subconscious (calm him down) ...**Sacred Code 1021

- **Smoking ...**Sacred Code 25543

- **Bipolar disorder...**Sacred Code 721

  - **Body Dysmorphic Disorder (Dysmorpho-phobia) ...**Sacred Code 818

- **Generalized development issue...**Sacred Code 81121
- **Borderline personality disorder...** Sacred Code 1630

- **Panic Disorder...**Sacred Code 1113

- **Mental disorder...**Sacred Code 488

- **Nervous Tics...**Sacred Code 829

- **Shyness...**Sacred Code 447

- **Sadness...**Sacred Code 770

- **Shame (unconscious)...**Sacred Code 72015

Improve personal appearance

- **Acne...** Sacred Code 879

- **Alopecia (Baldness) ...** Sacred Code 2574

- **Bags under the eyes ...** Sacred Code 2190

- **Dandruff...**Sacred Code 77216

- **Cellulitis...**Sacred Code 2911

- **Scars ...**Sacred Code 900900

- **Scalp...**Sacred Code 2080

- **Atopic dermatitis...**Sacred Code 123

- **Teeth in adults (New birth of) ...** Sacred Code 53123

- **Excess of Bello (hair) ...**Sacred Code 1594

- **Mushrooms...**Sacred Code 2679

- **Bunions ...**Sacred Code 3524

- **Spots on the skin...**Sacred Code 879

- **New Hair Birth ...**Sacred Code 394

- **Obesity...**Sacred Code 989

- **Skin (Strengthen the skin of the body)...** Sacred Code 459

- **Skin (For depigmentation)...**Sacred Code 515

- **Athlete's foot...**Sacred Code 67987
- **Skin Problems ...**Sacred Code 879

- **Weight (Lose From) ...**Sacred Code 32194

- **Weight (Do not climb) ...**Sacred Code 79418

- **Body Posture (Correct) ...**Sacred Code 679

- **Burns...**Sacred Code 25914

- **Seborrhea...**Sacred Code 511

- **Varicose ulcers...**Sacred Code 1917

- **Ingrown toenails...**Sacred Code 836

- **Varicose veins...**Sacred Code 71598

- **Warts ...**Sacred Code 31921

- **Vitiligo ...** Sacred Code 515

- **Swollen Body Areas ...**Sacred Code 578

Other health conditions

- **Achalasia ...**Sacred Code 2812

- **Uric acid (Lower) ...**Sacred Code 2050

- **CVA (cerebrovascular accident) ...**Sacred Code 1413

- **Activate telomerase ...**Sacred Code 80119

- **Activate Growth Hormone ...**Sacred Code 52611

- **Adenoids...**Sacred Code 11260

- **Aphonic (Stay) ...**Sacred Code 1570

- **Agenesis of the Corpus Callosum ...**Sacred Code 1179

- **Allergies ...**Sacred Code 572 and 1815

- **Dust Allergies ...**Sacred Code 68

- **Smoke Allergy ...**Sacred Code 37

- **Alopecia (baldness)** ...Sacred Code 2574

- **Amenorrhea** ...Sacred Code 754

- **Amoeba** ...Sacred Code 25

- **Tonsillitis**...Sacred Code 696

- **Amyloidosis** ...Sacred Code 790

- **Anemia**...Sacred Code 1111171 and 71521

- **Autism**...Sacred Code 6927
- **Aneurysm**...Sacred Code 2978

- **Appendix (Problems of)** ...Sacred Code 511

- **Excessive appetite** ...Sacred Code 551

- **Cardiac arrhythmia**...Sacred Code 2613

- **Wrinkles** ...Sacred Code 11112

- **Cerebellum Atrophy** ...Sacred Code 096

- **Frontal cortical atrophy** ...Sacred Code 72164

- **Type 2 spinal muscular atrophy ...** Sacred Code 31560

- **Bacteria in general ...**Sacred Code 1310

- **Clostridium bacteria ...**Sacred Code 2615

- **Proteus mirabilis bacteria ...**Sacred Code 1315

- **Bilirubin (normalization) ...**Sacred Code 721

- **Medulla oblongata (tumor) ...**Sacred Code 900

- **Bruxism ...**Sacred Code 568

- **Multinodular goiter...**Sacred Code 8116

- **Bursitis...**Sacred Code 25420

- **Headache)...**Sacred Code 428

- **Cadasil...**Sacred Code 22178

- **Cramps...**Sacred Code 2733

- **Calculations to the common bile duct...** Sacred Code 890

- **Kidney stones** ...Sacred Code 25809
- **Cancer...** Sacred Code 1577

- **Cancer in the brain** ... Sacred Code 499

- **Colon cancer...** Sacred Code 29700

- **Stomach cancer** ...Sacred Code 2111

- **Esophageal cancer** ...Sacred Code 620

- **Pharyngeal cancer** ... Sacred Code 1515

- **Cancer in the bones** ...Sacred Code 27900

- **Lymphoma Cancer** ...Sacred Code 25

- **Cancer nose** ...Sacred Code 211

- **Breast cancer** ...Sacred Code 53719

- **Pancreatic cancer...** Sacred Code 1328

- **Thyroid cancer...** Sacred Code 1180

- **Bladder cancer...**Sacred Code 1577

- **Testicular cancer...**Sacred Code 2194

- **Candidiasis ...**Sacred Code 894

- **Dilated Ischemic Cardipathy ...** Sacred Code 1619

- **Dandruff...**Sacred Code 77216

- **Cold and Cough ...**Sacred Code 611

- **Cavernomas ...**Sacred Code 2194

- **Cesarean section (to recover) ...**Sacred Code 579

- **Cysticercosis ...**Sacred Code 221
- **Cystitis...**Sacred Code 044

- **Sciatica...**Sacred Code 52037

- **Cirrhosis...**Sacred Code 88818

- **Cholesterol...**Sacred Code 900 and 72911

- **Colitis**...Sacred Code 81420

- **Ulcerative colitis** ...Sacred Code 81421

- **Ulcerative colitis**...Sacred Code 18

- **Coloboma in iris** ...Sacred Code 3851

- **Irritable Colon** ...Sacred Code 429

- **Menstrual cramps**...Sacred Code 82552

- **Induced coma**...Sacred Code 811

- **Contractures** ...Sacred Code 304

- **Chordoma in the brainstem** ... Sacred Code 7021

- **Chikungunya (to fight)** ...Sacred Code 515720

- **Craniopharyngioma** ...Sacred Code 1199

- **Craniosynostosis** ...Sacred Code 144521

- **Scalp**...Sacred Code 2080

- **Spring fingers** ...Sacred Code 2115

- **Dengue**...Sacred Code 1118

- **Dengue hemorrhagic fever** ...Sacred Code 2080

- **Atopic dermatitis**...Sacred Code 123
- **Dermatomyositis** ...Sacred Code 6153

- **Break**...Sacred Code 61271. This Code benefits the physical body.

- **Muscle Tear** ...Sacred Code 1121

- **Diarrhea**...Sacred Code 557

- **Dyslexia**...Sacred Code 11131

- **Cerebral dysrhythmia** ...Sacred Code 1543

- **Duchenne dystrophy** ...Sacred Code 57389

- **Fuchs' dystrophy** ...Sacred Code 31613

- **Heller's dystrophy** ...Sacred Code 715

- **Abdominal distension...**Sacred Code 421

- **Diverticulitis** ...Sacred Code 2828

- **Dyshidrosis (sweat blisters)** ...Sacred Code 89976

- **Abdominal distension...**Sacred Code 421

- **Dolores (any Nature)** ... Sacred Code 911

- **Headaches...**Sacred Code 199

- **Neuropathic pain...**Sacred Code 2023

- **Ebola (virus)** ...Sacred Code 556

- **Straighten teeth** ...Sacred Code 615

- **Eliminate tiredness (fatigue, wear, exhaustion)** ...Sacred Code 928

- **Contagious Diseases (break free)** ... Sacred Code 25300

- **Cohen's disease** ...Sacred Code 1615

- **Cuci's disease** ...Sacred Code 573

- **Gaucher disease** ...Sacred Code 1500

- **Hashimoto's disease** ...Sacred Code 2980

- **Peyronie's disease** ...Sacred Code 133

- **Heart valve diseases** ...Sacred Code 2060

- **Mental diseases**...Sacred Code 8977

- **Rendu Osler disease** ...Sacred Code 27500

- **Schamberg's disease** ...Sacred Code 2715

- **Waldenstrom's disease** ...Sacred Code 6093

- **Inflammation of the epididymis** ...Sacred Code 33

- **Pulmonary Emphysema** ...Sacred Code 75824

- **Embolisms** ...Sacred Code 621

- **Dental emergencies** ...Sacred Code 445

- **Epilepsy**...Sacred Code 753

- *Epidemic*...Sacred Code 66528

- **Scarlet fever**...Sacred Code 1180
- **Lateral sclerosis** ...Sacred Code 2114
- **Tuberous Sclerosis** ...Sacred Code 1615
- **Scoliosis**...Sacred Code 6579
- **Splenomegaly** ...Sacred Code 62316
- **Spondylolisthesis grade 2** ...Sacred Code 616
- **Constipation**...Sacred Code 1501
- **Sprains** ...Sacred Code 123
- **Calcaneal Spur** ...Sacred Code 44956
- **Stomach (discomfort)** ...Sacred Code 62139
- **Falcemia** ...Sacred Code 3110
- **Lack of appetite**...Sacred Code 316
- **Plantar fasciitis** ...Sacred Code 3336
- **Pulmonary fibrosis**...Sacred Code 62511
- **Fibrosis of the breasts** ...Sacred Code 1570

- **Typhoid fever...**Sacred Code 622

- **Skull fracture...**Sacred Code 8006

- **Fractures (that do not heal)...**Sacred Code 137

- **Intense cold (Normalize temperature)...**Sacred Code 211

- **Folliculitis...**Sacred Code 69
- **Strengthen weak tissues...**Sacred Code 62070

- **Boils...**Sacred Code 82913

- **Gangren...**Sacred Code 62014

- **Gastritis...**Sacred Code 44351

- **Stomach flu...**Sacred Code 0839

- **Gastroenterocolitis...**Sacred Code 6128

- **Flu...**Sacred Code 630

- **Gases...**Sacred Code 511

- **Hits**...Sacred Code 621

- **Gout**...Sacred Code 120

- **Halitosis**...Sacred Code 27600

- **Hemochromatosis** ...Sacred Code 601

- **Hemophilia**...Sacred Code 31200

- **Hemorrhoids**...Sacred Code 2579

- **Hepatosplenomegaly** ...Sacred Code 2190

- **Wounds** ...Sacred Code 518

- **Congenital Diaphragmatic Hernia** ...Sa-grade code 92

- **Herniated Discs** ...Sacred Code 52130

- **Herniated Disc** ...Sacred Code 711

- **Inguinal hernia**...Sacred Code 1525

- **Lumbosacral hernia** ...Sacred Code 79

- **Umbilical Hernia …**Sacred Code 2082

- **Brain Hemangiomas …**Sacred Code 373

- **Herpes…**Sacred Code 52751

- **Genital herpes…**Lumbosacral Hernia: 79 Sacred Code 2728

- **Herpes zoster…**Sacred Code 27500

- *Hepatitis…*Sacred Code 82976

- **Bleeding (to stop) …**Sacred Code 82971

- **Hydrocephalus …**Sacred Code 62100

- **Dropsy…**Sacred Code 61800

- **Hidradenitis…**Sacred Code 921

- **Idiopathic Hirsutism …**Sacred Code 21504

- **Hyperhidrosis…**Sacred Code 58750

Pulmonary Arterial Hypertension…25300

54722

- **Endometrial Hyperplasia** ...Sacred Code 7114

- **Adrenal Hyperplasia** ...Sacred Code 2914

- **Hyperthyroidism** ... Sacred Code 293

- **Hiccup**...Sacred Code 828

- **Hearing loss** ...Sacred Code 600
- **Hypocalcemia** ...Sacred Code 2120

- **Hypoglycemia** ...Sacred Code 1570

- **Hypoplasia** ...Sacred Code 65728

- **Hypothyroidism** ...Sacred Code 1966

- **Hypotonia** ...Sacred Code 1574

- **Mushrooms**...Sacred Code 2679

- **Influenza**...Sacred Code 259

- **Fecal Incontinence** ...Sacred Code 27315

- **Urinary incontinence** ...Sacred Code 52524

- **Intestinal inflammation ...**Sacred Code 874 and 225

- **Urinary infections...**Sacred Code 3334

- **Renal insufficiency...**Sacred Code 213

- **Harelip...**Sacred Code 820

- **Lactose (Intolerance) ...**Sacred Code 21300

- **Brain and neurological injuries ...**Sacred Code 87031

- **Injuries to the Corpus Callosum ...**Sacred Code 212

- **Spinal cord injury...**Sacred Code 2115

- **Leukemia...**Sacred Code 583

- **Lymphedema ...**Sacred Code 1193

- **Hodgkin lymphoma ...**Sacred Code 1021

- **Sores inside the mouth ...**Sacred Code 1199
- **Sores on the body ...**Sacred Code 5794

- **Rotator cuff**...Sacred Code 1112

- **Genetic malformations** ...Sacred Code 6234

- **Dizziness** ...Sacred Code 759 and 615

- **Meningitis**...Sacred Code 2599

- **Cancer metastasis** ...Sacred Code 690

- **Transverse myelitis**...Sacred Code 2231

- **Migraines** ...Sacred Code 67918

- **Leg mobility** ...Sacred Code 1613

- **New hair birth** ...Sacred Code 394

- **Nerves**...Sacred Code 827

- **Pneumothorax**...Sacred Code 6944

- **Neuralgia**...Sacred Code 613

- **Peripheral neuropathy** ...Sacred Code 21402

- **Pneumonia**...Sacred Code 1775

- **Vocal cord nodules ...** Sacred Code 27604

- **Throat Nodules ...**Sacred Code 2190

- **Breast nodules ...**Sacred Code 20

- **Nodules in the lung ...**Sacred Code 3634

- **Nodules in the liver ...**Sacred Code 27504

- **Obesity...**Sacred Code 989
- **Smell (to get it back)...**Sacred Code 429

- **Respiratory oppressions ...**Sacred Code 814

- **Osteopenia...**Sacred Code 617 and 11125

- **Degenerative Osteoarthritis...**Sacred Code 11834

- **Facial paralysis...**Sacred Code 879

- **Parasites...**Sacred Code 511

- **Paresthesia...**Sacred Code 1639

- **Physical paralysis...**Sacred Code 10222

- **Pemphigus...** Sacred Code 329

- **Ocular scar pemphigoid...** Sacred Code 285

- **Peristalsis ...** Sacred Code 657

- **Body Weight (problems)...** Sacred Code 32194

- **Weight (do not climb)...** Sacred Code 79418

- **Stings...** Sacred Code 701

- **Athlete's foot...** Sacred Code 67987

- **Skin (Depigmentation of)...** Sacred Code 515

- **Body Skin (Strengthen)...** Sacred Code 459

- **Lice...** Sacred Code 10120
- **Polycythemia Rubra Vera ...** Sacred Code 612

- **Polymyalgia rheumatica...** Sacred Code 281

- **Body Posture (correct) ...** Sacred Code 679

- **Polyps (Colon and Rectum) ...**Sacred Code 58519
- **High pressure...**Sacred Code 54721
- **Low pressure...**Sacred Code 11561
- **Bronchial Problems ...**Sacred Code 506
- **Circulatory problems ...**Sacred Code 52311
- **Intestinal problems...**Sacred Code 628
- **Neurological problems ...**Sacred Code 827
- **Dental problems ...**Sacred Code 2914
- **Palate problems ...**Sacred Code 1340
- **Respiratory problems...**Sacred Code 443
- **Prolactin ...**Sacred Code 856
- **Vaginal prolapse ...**Sacred Code 2133
- **Prostatitis...**Sacred Code 5533 and 33
- **Proteus mirabilis ...**Sacred Code 1315

- **Psoriasis...**Sacred Code 82074
- **Pulpitis...**Sacred Code 1974

- **Enoch Purple ...**Sacred Code 2820
- **Sebaceous cysts ...**Sacred Code 1211

- **Thyroid cyst...**Sacred Code 670

- **Burns (in general) ...**Sacred Code 25914

- **Body Itch (itch) ...**Sacred Code 119

  - **Reduction of the dimensions of the skull...** Sacred Code 2139

- **Gastric reflux...**Sacred Code 26700

- **Regenerate cartilage in joints...**Sacred Code 2929

- **Insulin Regulation...**Sacred Code 22573

- **Pelvic Floor Rehabilitation...**Sacred Code 9911

- **Common cold...**Sacred Code 2710

- **Insulin resistance ...**Sacred Code 22573

- **Restore body collagen...**Sacred Code 2831
- **Food Restrictions (Alleviate Situation)...** Sacred Code 14

- **Mental retardation...**Sacred Code 524

- **Rhinitis...**Sacred Code 884

- **Snoring...**Sacred Code 2870
- **Rosacea ...**Sacred Code 53357

  - **Healing (accelerating processes at all levels)...**Numerical Sacred Code 128

- **Brain Healing and Strengthening...**Sacred Code 218

- **Healing of Sexuality...**Sacred Code 843

- **Excessive and profuse salivation...** Sacred Code 2123

- **Seborrhea...**Sacred Code 51

- **Tooth sensitivity...**Sacred Code 2179

- **Septicemia**...Sacred Code 6152

- **Deafness**...Sacred Code 721
- **Chilblains** ...Sacred Code 62030

- **Alstrom Hallgren syndrome**...Sacred Code 630

- **Asperger syndrome**...Sacred Code 50310

- **Down's Syndrome**...Sacred Code 418

- **Guillian Barré syndrome** ...Sacred Code 72080

- **Job syndrome** ...Sacred Code 71950

- **Meniere's syndrome** ...Sacred Code 80808

- **Sturge Weber syndrome**...Sacred Code 11

- **Vacterl syndrome** ...Sacred Code 36

- **Von Hippel Lindau syndrome** ...Sacred Code 279

- **Sinusitis**...Sacred Code 72120

- **AIDS**...Sacred Code 41188

- **Stiff person syndrome...**Sacred Code 820
- **Restless Leg Syndrome...** Sacred Code 6818

- **Deep and restful sleep ...**Sacred Code 2820

- **Thalassemia...**Sacred Code 3110

- **Stutterers...**Sacred Code 28500

- **Stammering...**Sacred Code 1611

- **Telangiectasias ...**Sacred Code 115

- **Tendinitis ...**Sacred Code 11226

- **Chronic tendinosis (shoulders)...** Sacred Code 72915

- **Ovarian Teratoma ...**Sacred Code 1218

- **Shyness...**Sacred Code 447

- **Tinnitus ...**Sacred Code 690

- **Toxoplasmosis...**Sacred Code 1613

- **Bone marrow transplant...**Sacred Code 6314

- **Kidney Transplants...**Sacred Code 901

- **Triglycerides and Cholesterol ...**Sacred Code 72911

- **Thrombosis...**Sacred Code 681

- **Tuberculosis...**Sacred Code 29701

- **Tumors (Keep them from growing) ...**Sacred Code 16404

- **Brain tumor...**Sacred Code 55211

- **Cranial tumor ...**Sacred Code 1614

- **Carpal tunnel...**Sacred Code 1570

- **Stomach ulcers ...**Sacred Code 3726

- **Stomach ulcers ...**Sacred Code 62315

- **Varicose ulcers...**Sacred Code 1917

- **Ingrown toenails...**Sacred Code 836

- **Urticaria...**Sacred Code 62071

- **Uveitis ...**Sacred Code 6050
- **Chickenpox...**Sacred Code 67112

- **Warts ...**Sacred Code 31921

- **HPV (human papillomavirus) ...**Sacred Code 10160

- **Vertigo...**Sacred Code 31576

- **Gallbladder (problems) ...**Sacred Code 801000

- **Zika virus ...**Sacred Code 8090

- **Vitiligo ...**Sacred Code 515

- **Vomiting ...**Sacred Code 112
- **Buzzing ...**Sacred Code 774

- **Swollen areas of the body ...**Sacred Code 578

Medications, doctors and surgeries

- **Clots after surgical intervention ...**Sacred Code 718

- **Eliminate drug side effects ...** Sacred Code 2929

- **Success in surgery ...**Sacred Code 42716

- **Releasing medications from adverse effects** ...Sacred Code 533

- **Free yourself from surgical intervention** ...Sacred Code 55726. Sometimes surgery can cause inconveniences in a person's life. This Code invokes the angelic magic of the Archangel Ra-fael who is qualified to grant these kinds of gifts.

- **Get rid of bad doctors ...**Sacred Code 61

- **Getting rid of surgery ...**Sacred Code 8092. More than one of those who will read this message are afraid of undergoing surgery, due to misfortunes in this regard. This number will get ridof it.

- **To attract organ donors ...** Sacred Code 527

The Person and His Circumstances, Animals and Planets

Colors

- **Purple...**Sacred Code 27

- **Blue...**Sacred Code 18

- **Green...**Sacred Code 91

- **Yellow...**Sacred Code 11

- **Golden...**Sacred Code 77

- **Red...**Sacred Code 29

- **Orange...**Sacred Code 15

- **Pinkish...**Sacred Code 8

- **White...**Sacred Code 100

- **Black...**Sacred Code 2

Weekdays

- **Monday...**Sacred Code 47

- **Tuesday...**Sacred Code 69

- **Wednesday...**Sacred Code 104

- **Thursday...**Sacred Code 25

- **Friday...**Sacred Code 71

- **Saturday...**Sacred Code 93

- **Sunday...**Sacred Code 156

Houses

- **Access to a new house or dwelling...**Sacred Code 171717. There are many Souls eager to move toanother place and breathe new air.

- **Attract a buyer for your home...**Sacred Code 515

- **Change residence or city (Be close to)...**Sacred Code 413

- **Finding the right person when renting a property...**Sacred Code 82412. This Code is very important, because through it we will attract a person with a good vibration and who will pay the monthly payments in full.

- **Moisture and fungi in homes...**Sacred Code 1

- **Moving to a new home...**Sacred Code 715

- **To move house...**Sacred Code 72988

- **To buy a house...**Sacred Code 52574

- **To successfully negotiate your assets...** Sacred Code 2194. A considerable percentage of you wish to negotiate your Heritage. Through this

Number they will get in touch with the perfect client to carry out the appropriate transactions successfully.

- **To sell a house...**Sacred Code 105

- **Sell or quickly change your properties...**Sacred Code 181818. Many of those who read these words want to sell or exchange their goods, because their Soul wants to open up to new environments and opportunities.

- **Know where to move before selling a house...**Sacred code 569. This Number is useful in the following case: Suppose you have the place where you live for sale. This Code shows you the place where you should move in advance. So when they sell, they already know where to go. Can be combined with code 715

- **Annoying and noisy neighbors...**Sacred Code 221

Business

- **Affine Soul for business...** Sacred Code 0799. There are many people who need a good company tohelp them run their business. It is not about a part- ner, Merlin refers to a kindred soul who, in addition to loving us, helps us to soften the load of each day. Between the two of you, things are more bearable. Merlin offers the Code so that he will come to help ussoon.

- **Angel Anauel...**Sacred Code 379. He is the Angelof business and businessmen.

- **Attract customers to a business...**Sacred Code 71588

- **Prevent them from setting up a business...** Sacred Code 52537. Avoid installing inconvenient businesses or establishments in a neighborhood.

- **Judas Thaddeus...**Sacred Code 16700 and 45600. In its aspect of successful negotiations.

- **Business...**Sacred Code 105

- **Buying and selling businesses...**Sacred Code 52574 and 71521

- **To ask for a mentor in the business area...**
  Sacred Code 72911

Abundance and prosperity

- **Open yourself to new opportunities...**Sacred Code 1111

- **Open paths...**Sacred Code 691

- **Abundance...**Sacred Code 194

- **Abundance...**Sacred Code 8829, 375, 684, 424, 299, 874, 1697, 531, 889 and 912. Received from san expedito.

  - **Accelerate the advent of wealth into your life...**Sacred Code 133

- **Angel of abundance...**Sacred Code 71269. I want to help you discover your hidden treasures, I want to help you so that prosperity and joy flow in your lives. When you feel that agonizing anguish caused by not having enough money, give me a call.

- **Angels of Well-being...**Sacred Code 607

- **Angel Giria...**Sacred Code 1191. Expert in everything related to money

- **Angel of Wealth**...Sacred Code 88829. It is an entity that wishes to help you solve your financial problems. His energy is very close to that of the Archangel Gabriel and Mother Mary.

- **Angel Parasiel**...Sacred Code 515. This Angel prepares the way to abundance.

- **Erimihala's help in meditation from abundance**...Sacred Code 194. Quietly but firmly begin to repeat the Sacred Code 194. If you remain attentive you will notice my energy, and you will perceive that I AM THINKING THROUGH YOU. This will greatly facilitate viewing. Your share of work is to repeat the Sacred Code and focus on PICTURES OF ABUNDANCE that I myself will inspire. If you work with the above Code, you will see very rapid changes.

  - **Connection with the Elemental of Money** ...Sacred Code 47620.

- **When someone owes you money and doesn't want to pay you**...Sacred Code 858. This invokes the energy of Saint Anthony of Padua, who is the recoverer of lost assets.

- **Money (for the money to arrive)**...Sacred Code 897

- Goddess Lakshmi...Sacred Code 2918. The God-sa of wealth and beauty. It is believed that all those who adore her know immediate happiness. Dissolve and root out implants that pre- vent connection with the Energy of Money ...Sacred Code 61316, 541280, and 73016.

  When there is an implant, no matter how good willit be, the result of visualizations and decrees is poor. So the key is to remove those implants so that the sit-uation is favorable. Mother Mary in her Advocation or Aspect of Our Lady of the Sacred Heart, and Mas-ter Kwan Yin, offer these three codes.

- **Success at work ...**Sacred Code 643

- **Planetary Genius OCH ...**Sacred Code 1016. It governs the affairs of the Sun. It teaches medicine, wisdom, and gives money. He has 36,536 Spirits at his service, and he sends them according to the needs of each one. It is done on Sunday.

- **Obtaining Additional Sources of Income** ...Sacred Code 904

- **To find a job (Specify which one)...**Sacred Code 454545, 16700 and 5600 (any of the 3).

- **For the money to flow to you...**Sacred Code 1122 and 5701

- **So that the money they need arrives smoothly...**Sacred Code 42170

- **Financial problems: (Deliver concerns to God)...**Sacred Code 608

- **Prosperity...**Sacred Code 79

- **Gifts from the Universe (receive)...**Sacred Code 545 and 32300

- **Remove from their Energy Field the spirits of ruin and misery...ISUMI TALASI. Word of the sacred language of Ageon to combine with the...**Sacred Code 773.

- **Favorable trip...**Sacred Code 100. Through this Number the Beings of Light can help us to have a favorable trip. This implies that the vehicle in which we are going works well, and does not suffer any setback.

It is important to do our part to align ourselves with the successful journey. If the Code is made and at the same time it is thought that a tire is going to explode, for example, we are interfering with the success of theprocess.

Human relations

- **Soulmate (to facilitate this connection)...**Sacred Code 571

- **Friendships (Good and New)...**Sacred Code 1129

- **Love as a couple (Strengthen it)...**Sacred Code 541

- **Universal love...**Sacred Code 35133

- **Attract kindred souls (As Friendship)...**Sacred Code 12000

- **Attract kindred souls (As a life partner)...** Code Sacred 715400

- **Attract love...**Sacred Code 2526

- **Attract the love of your life...**Sacred Code 11550. By using this number many will be healed of their loneliness, and they will know that enjoying a beautiful company benefits their physical and mental health.

-

- **Quickly attract your Life Companion or Companion...**Sacred Code 191919. Good company brings joy and prosperity, and many of you are in need of it. This means that your Soul yearns to experience this healthy union.

- **Jealousy...**Sacred Code 1015

- **Keeping good friends...**Sa-grade code 725

- **Infidelity...**Sacred Code 212

- **Thought projection at a distance...** Sacred Code 580. This projection to which I refer is proposed, not imposed. Through this Code you can address the Soul of any person, and it is transpersonal, that is, it goes beyond the ego. Once they have chosen the appropriate person, sitting or lying down they will make a verbalization similar or equal to this: Through the Sacred Code 580 I bring to my mind... and I imagine him as if he were with me. Then begin to pass the beads on the necklace by counting: 580 (one), 580 (two), 580 (three) and make the mental picture of the person as real as possible while continuing to count.

- Etheric Retreat of the Archangel Chamuel...Sacred Code 725. Whoever wants to receive stim- ulating energy and unexpected surprises, ask his Soul to lead him at night, to the etheric retreat of the Archangel Chamuel. This Being frees the cap- tive, and handles the area of relationships at all levels. His name means "God is my Goal." Thanks to the intervention of this Archangel, relationshipsthat have been broken for years can be reestab- lished. Whoever feels unloved or rejected, will findin Chamuel the best confidant and friend. Uncomfortable relationships (break free)...Sacred Code 28

- **Loneliness...**Numerical Sacred Code 11136

Protection

- **Accidents (break free)...**Sacred Code 748

- **Sexual harassment...**Sacred Code 22211

- **Get away early from a place where we no longer want to be...**Sacred Code 188

- **Lighten legal procedures...**Sacred Code 627

- **Alternatives when the picture is confusing...**Sacred Code 718. To raise alternatives. Offered by Ruth and Cristina de Andrómeda.

- **Assaults (get off)...**Sacred Code 697

- **Cancer (to preventively protect against this disease and prevent it from reaching them)...**Sacred Code 1188

- **Unfair charge...**Sacred Code 125512. This is applied in the event that they are making us "an unfair bribe". It can be a sum of money that someone, whoever they are, is charging us. For example, a tax that has been paid in a state entity and we do not owe it.

- **Against accidents...**Sacred Code 41404

- **Cutting of Telepathic Ties...**Sacred Code 577. There are ties that bind us to other people and from which it is necessary to free ourselves. These bindings come from other lives and continue to influence us today. Through this Code we free ourselves from telepathic influence ethics that such entities exert on us and we eliminate any trace or record that may remain in our psyche.

- **Guilt (feeling free from)...**Sacred Code 339

- **Clear paths...**Sacred Code 75139. This is a Master number by means of which you will crush the head of the serpent, and your ways will be cleared.

- **Egrégoras (Protection)...**Sacred Code 1611. The energies of the Egregoras intoxicate people with weak minds.

- **Emergency...**Sacred Code 594, 677, 525 and 437 Urgent problems of all kinds that need to be solved and they cannot find a way to do it. Offered by Ruth of Andromeda for emergency help.

- **Competent and Honest Domestic Service Employees...**Sacred Code 16700

- **Finding lost things...**Sacred Code 858 and 725

- **Hidden Enemies (get rid of)...**Sacred Code 051

- **Deception (get rid of)...**Sacred Code 3351

- **Anger (Ignore)...**Sacred Code 11139. (Generally people use anger in front of others as a means of manipulation, intimidation, or provocation. With this Code we ignore those energies, preventing them from affecting us).

- **Envy (to protect yourself)...**Sacred Code 615

- **Mocking Spirits (break free)...**Sacred Code 314

- **Spirits of ruin and misery (break free)...** Sacred Code 773. Thus they will clean and prepare the ground, so that the angels Gabriel, Parasiel and Abun-dia, can sow seeds of abundance).

- **Being at peace in a temporary place that you don't want to be...**Sacred Code 1679. A good number of you are in places where you do not want to be, and your stay there is temporary. Through this Number you will be able to live in peace there, while it is time to leave.

- **Avoid damage from neighbors...**Sacred Code 530

- **Frustration (break free)...**Sacred Code 6279

- **Sinister forces (protection)...**Sacred Code 455

- **Great misfortunes (break free)...**Sacred Code 339

- **Prevent anyone from hurting you or taking advantage of you...**Sacred Code 11129. Whether it is family, friends, or any other kind of relationship.

- **Astral larvae and implants...**Sacred Code 1118

- **Misfortune (Get rid of)...**Sacred Code 2000

- **Summon the spirit of home...**Sacred Code 715

- **Justice (When you feel that an injustice is being committed)...**Sacred Code 3128, 32328, 33319, 33486, 33529, 33657 and 33894. Sources: Ruth and Cristina de Andrómeda.

- **Thieves (Against)...**Sacred Code 781

- **Get rid of E.T's shares...**Sacred Code 401

- **Get rid of any natural or legal person that is hindering them in any way...**Sacred Code 42 and 892. They will be free of it.

- **Get rid of contagious diseases...**Sacred Code 25300

- **Get rid of implants...**Sacred Code 575, 26, 104 and 1679. There is a type of "implant" that can only be canceled by means of the Sacred Codes, I am referring to a vibrational barrier that I would call "of failure", so to speak and adjusting to yourlanguage. Many feel disappointed, sad, and be- wildered, because they are stagnant and unable to shake off their visible and invisible oppressors.

  Despite your valiant efforts, there is something that does not allow you to be free, although you feel the comfort and the beneficent breeze of your Angels and Guides.

- **Get rid of the feeling of being in a hurry or in a hurry...**Sacred Code 52579

- **Get rid of advantageous people (who try totake advantage of the good faith of others for their interests)...**Sacred Code 483

- **Get rid of evil spirits...**Sacred Code 12900

- **Free people from black magic...**Sacred Code 8585

- **Get rid of works of black magic...**Sacred Code 111 111 111

- **Get rid of the paralyzing feeling of stagnation...**Sacred Code 860. It mobilizes energies of Saturn so that the time yields in the work and daily activities.

- **Cleanse the aura...**Sacred Code 26700

- **Negative cleanings...**Sacred Code 0927. To clean spaces of vibrations, objects, people, and negative entities of all kinds. This number is like a broom that sweeps away all the trash that can harm us. It can be used for the home, the office, or any place where we enter and that we feel with bad energy.

- **Wrong place (to leave)...**Sacred Code 997. This Code is effective for people who feel they are in "the wrong place". It can give them benefits, as they come to a new place where their talents are appreciated and recognized.

- **The evil eye...**Sacred Code 69900. This is real, in the same way that "black magic" is real. The eyes, as they have heard so many times are the windows of the soul. From the eyes come magnetic effluvia, energy currents, capable of influencing the minds of people. When someone envies you, hates you, or simply does not love you, it sends out those effluvia causing damage inside. That is why we have insisted so much on Protections.

- **Afraid...**Sacred Code 680

- **Don't be caught off guard...**Sacred Code 593

- **Obtain collaboration from the Authorities...** Sacred Code 534. It goes without saying that it is for lawful causes.

- **To take care of our belongings...**Code Sa- cred 1198. Here I am not referring to the heritagewhose Code I have already delivered. It alludes tothe things and objects that we appreciate and that accompany us in daily life: House decorations, objects for personal use that we like, beautiful memories that we keep.

- **In order not to be so sensitive to noise...**Sacred Codes 1651419, 2739, 883. There are Souls with a wonderful sensitivity who do not tolerate noise. This Code can alleviate them relatively.

- **For people who have Negative Entities attached to their Bodies...**Sacred Code 1221 and

316. This causes them much suffering. Cristina de Andrómeda has revealed two Codes for these people.

- **For spiteful people...**Sacred Code 2888

  - **To protect yourself from physical attacks...** Sacred Code 1025

- **To have peace around...**Sacred Code 300600. Every time you need to have peace around, repeat this Code.

- **Stray people...**Sacred Code 29700

- **Kidnapped people...**Sacred Code 520

- **Pests (Delete)...**Sacred Code 1618

- **Protection and assistance in case of earthquakes...**Sacred Code 479 and 484. Offered by Mother Mary in her invocation of Our Lady of The Miraculous Medal.

- **Protection against accidents...**Sacred Code 804
- **Protection against karmic enemies...**Sacred Code 314

- **UV protection**...Sacred Code 2016

- **Protection against black magic works**...Sacred Code 1617. Offered by Ascended Master Kwan Yin. As Jesus and Babaji have said, this exists, and it is very harmful to Souls.

- **Heritage protection**...Sacred Code 899751

- **Protect yourself (from harmful radiation of any kind)**...Sacred Code 333444

- **To nullify harmful energies**...Sacred Code 618, The Souls that are noticing a drop in their energies and are confused. Do not have the slightest fear, because this is an underground action of dark forces that are desperate for the rapid expansion of light.

- **Remove interference from the lower astral**...Sacred Code 237

- **Reinforce cancellation of voluntary agreement** ...Sacred Code 017 and 018. You will see how the beings who have not respected their decision to cancel the agreements of wills, will lose their power, and will not be able to continue mistreating them or subtracting their vital energy.

- **Repair damage to the aura** ...Sacred Code 811

- **Remove a person who does not comply with our activity** ...Sacred Code 5721. This Code is to ask the Beings of Light to withdraw from our activity a person with whom we have made an agreement of wills, and he does not fulfill his part.

  - **Get our opponents out of the Energy field**...Sacred Code 694

  - **Leaving a place where you don't want to be...** Sacred Code 72988

- **Healings (Restore and protect)** ...Sacred Code 33351 Ascended Master Kwan Yin Code, in case of damage.

- **Healer** ...Sacred Code 44. Act in form effective and powerful, in all their bodies, root out captive aftermath by attacks of "black magic" in the past and today.

- **Security**...Sacred Code 0000000

- **Seal their auras** ...Sacred Code 19-9-1913. Coming from the divine Light of the Planet AGEON, and that seals your auras against the work that the Asyntrions (Beings of Darkness) have done on you, your loved ones, and your benefactors. In this Code, in addition to me, Mother Mary and Master Saint Germain participate.

- **Be careful in case of tremors ...**Sacred Code 10894. Whoever recites this Code will be taken care of together with his house in case of earthquakes.

- **To be freed from karmic oppressors who have as neighbors ...**Sacred Code 119. Those whouse this code will be freed from karmic oppressors that they have as neighbors, and that with their noise and rudeness alter their quality of life.

- **Desperate situations ...**Sacred Code 19

- **Withstand high temperatures ...**Code Sagrade 111

  - **Finish breaking uncomfortable Telepathic Ties...**Sacred Code 151515

- **Traps and deceptions...**Sacred Code 816

- **Energetic Vampires (Avoid Encounters)...** Sacred Code 441. An energetic vampire has a dysfunc- tional inner energy system. At the Having an energy deficiency and impaired energy systems, they feed off the energy of other people. An energy vampire attack can occur during physical contact, by shaking hands, or at great distances.

- **"Energetic vampirism" or psychic ...**Sacred Code 7000. You already know that these people have deteriorated energy systems, and they feed on the energy of other people.

- **Domestic Violence ...**Sacred Code 820

Personal and spiritual improvement

- **Open paths...**Sacred Code 691

- **Open yourself to new opportunities...**Sa-grade code 1111

- **Accelerate the vibration of the body to-wards higher planes...**Sacred Code 659

- **Acquiring practical sense...**Sacred Code 1714

- **Lightening of ascension symptoms...**Sa-cred Code 680

- **Soul...**Sacred Code 4500000 (communicate, it will tell you what resonates with your inner truth).

- **Souls addicted to suffering...**Sacred Code 7278. These people reject everything that can bring them joy, and they always have a reason to feel bad.

- **Self-love...**Sacred Code 877

- **Learn to control your own mind...**Sacred Code 85

- **Self boycott...**Sacred Code 593. The fear of success can be experienced by anyone at some pointin their life.

- **Self-control and Discipline...**Sacred Code 26200

- **Self esteem...**Sacred Code 877

- **Self-control...**Sacred Code 784

- **Bilocation...**Sacred Code 61522. Simultaneous presence of a person in two different places.

- **Close Cycles...**Code 10845

- **Brain...**Sacred Code 10-24-1975. With the power of Mataji and the Ascended Master Saint Germain, I make operative all those areas of my brain that have been inactive for a long time. By Divine Order, they now go into action for the Glory of the Divine spirit

- **Concentration...**Sacred Code 00

- **Compassion...**Sacred Code 9999

- **Connect with double...**Sacred Code 682. The Double is yourself, but in another Dimension. It is that part of you that remained on your Planet of origin when you incarnated.

- **Get the most pressing wish we have...**Sacred Code 25700. Offered by Master Kwan Yin.

- **Control the mind ...**Sacred Code 39: Sometimes it is difficult for a number of reasons, This Code is precisely for that.

- **Creativity (unlock) ...**Sacred Code 18357

- **When you need someone's support ...**Sacred Code 917 and 868

- **Detachment...**Sacred Code 986 and 1218

- **Develop positive emotions...**Sacred Code 578. Why is it difficult to manifest our dreams ?, Because the emotional component does not have enough strength to materialize the desire.

  Through this Code we will strengthen "Positive emotion", which will allow dreams to come true.

- **Develop assertiveness ...**Sacred Code 464

- **Develop self-confidence ...**Sacred Code 451

- **Development of Telepathy** ...Sacred Code 19813

- **Unlock the inner voice** ...Sacred Code 563. There are many souls who, despite achieving internal silence, do not listen to anything. This Code is for them.

- **Discover and set your own color**...Sacred Code 12579

- **Despair**...Sacred Code 19

- **Awaken generosity**...Sacred Code 78

- **Awaken the dormant and blocked imagination**...Sacred Code 899

- **Discernment**...Sacred Code 555

- **Start and Finish a Project**...Sacred Code 211

- **Finding lost things**...Sacred Code 858 and 725

- **Anger**...Sacred Code 11139. To ignore the anger of others, Generally people use anger in front of others as a means of manipulation, intimidation, or provocation. With this Code, we ignore these energies, preventing them from affecting us.

- **Listen to our interior...**Sacred Code 113

- **Hear the true inner voice...**Sacred Code 431 and 1155

- **Success...**Sacred Code 2190

- **Facilitate the learning of new languages...** Sacred Code 529

  Faith... Sacred Code 32,414 and 504

- **Faith, courage, consolation, and total help (Te-ner)...**Sacred Code 780. Sent by Mother Mary in her invocation of Our Lady of The Miraculous Medal

- **Frustrations (Break free)...**Sacred Code 6279

- **Phobias...**Sacred Code 66 and 32

  - **Intense cold as a symptom of ascension...** Sacred Code 211

- **Gratitude...**Sacred Code 3333

- **Make our destiny more bearable...**Sacred Code 37. If you do this Code you will notice peace and relaxation.

- **Modesty**...Sacred Code 11

- **Uncertainty (Alleviate)**...Sacred Code 27

- **Intelligence (increase)**...Sacred Code 1523

- **Interpret unfamiliar scripts, symbols, and languages** ...Sacred Code 19996

- **Interpret the signs**...Sacred Code 2615. There are subtle, camouflaged signs.

- **Intuition**...Sacred Code 811

- **Release from confusion**...Sacred Code 808. There are many people who feel confused in many areas, and do not know what decision to make. Through this Number the whole picture is clarified.

- **Maintain the balance between the spiritual and the material**...Sacred Code 69. There are people who ignore the spiritual world, and others who ignore the material world. Attunement with both is necessary. You have to have contact with both worlds.

- **Improve singing skills**...Sacred Code 52088

- **Memory**...Sacred Code 574

- **Afraid**...Sacred Code 680

- **Miracles**...Sacred Code 4418 and 1913. Offered by Merlin to obtain miracles.

- **Multiply signals**...Sacred Code 62413

- **Identifier Number** Use your birthday date (mm / dd / yyyy)

- **Internal Child (Communication with the**healthy part) ...**Sacred Code 879. This is vital, because the inner child knows our truth, andknows what our mission is.**

- **Inner Child (Reconcile with)** ...Sacred Code 89

- **Wounded Inner Child (Heal)** ...Sacred Code 991

- **Inner Child (Heal)** ...Sacred Code 3740

- **Inner Child (Virtues)** ...Sacred Code 344

- **Patience...**Sacred Code 629

- **People who do not feel free ...**Sacred Code 906. Through this number you will experience freedom.

- **Peace all around ...**Sacred Code 959

- **Sorry...**Sacred Code 888

- **Ask for advice or receive signals ...** Sacred Code 484

- **Ask for advice and be helped by this ...**Sacred Code 456

- **People who are terrified of the future ...** Sacred Code 378. It helps and exercises a calming action on the person who uses it.

- **Set limits (learn) ...**Sacred Code 728

- **Rage...**Sacred Code 201

- **Receive specific information for your individual process...**Sacred Code 00991. Whoever uses this Number with faith, and is relaxed and attentive, will receive information from Merlin, which can be very revealing.

- **Remember dreams...**Sacred Code 2137

- **Taking an exam**...Sacred Code 32511

- **Conscious Breathing**...Sacred Code 2500. This single action will anchor you in the present, it will connect permanently with us

- **Regain inner power** ...Sacred Code 62987

- **Secrets and Hidden Things**...Sacred Code 2020. Through it secrets and hidden things will be revealed to you. They can also call it the Code of Speed, because it will manifest very quickly what they dream of.

- **Feeling of unworthiness (Heal)**...Sacred Code 593 and 294. This state of mind is fatal for success, since the person who suffers from it is imprisoned in the false belief of "not deserving anything". The aforementioned sensation works on a subconscious level and is firmly ingrained in many people.

- **Overreaction (Avoid)** ...Sacred Code 520. Sometimes you overreact to difficulties, and this is somewhat exhausting.

- **Loneliness**...Sacred Code 11136

- **Request the literal signs** ...Sacred Code 373 and 418. These are forceful and unmistakable. The

LITERAL signal can be received in the dream while we sleep, or in the middle of daily activity.

- **Subconscious (calm the)** ...Sacred Code 1021. The painful events of this and other lives are stored in the subconscious, so that when an event occurs that contains some discomfort or sadness, similar repressed material is precipitated, giving rise to anguish and restlessness. Whenever you feel bad, with obsessive, sad, or overly sensitive ideas, let yourself be lulled by the magic of this Code and you will experience the serenity of the mind.

- **Tranquillity**...Sacred Code 0129

- **Sadness**...Sacred Code 770

- **Tolerance**...Sacred Code 665

- **Travels**...Sacred Code 681

- **Conscious Astral Travel** ...Sacred Code 729

- **Will (Strengthen)** ...Sacred Code 574

Past and present lives of self andfamily

- **Family Tree (to heal)...**Sacred Code 553

- **Pending issues...**Sacred Code 791. Through this code, repressed material from the past (this and other lives) comes to light that prevents us from moving freely and agilely.

  - **Erase negative memories from the subconscious...**Sacred Code 45600

- **Cancellation of Karmic Bonds...**Sacred Code 14710 and 1579. Given by Uriel Arcángel.

- **Episodes from previous lives...**Sacred Code 623. Through this number Elyasim shows us fragments of previous existences that need to be healed.

- **Listen to the me of the past ...**Sacred Code 000

- **Holy Spirit...**Sacred Code 443355. Liberation from many karmic ties and oppressors that have made your life difficult during several incarnations including the current one. This liberation is possible thanks to the presence of the one you know as the Holy Spirit.

- **Painful experiences with people close to you in the present (Heal)...**Sacred Code 812. You have been disturbed in some way in the past. Negative feelings towards someone they are not "free". They have a reason for being, and generally it is a matter of other lives. There are beings that produce discomfort, stress, and sometimes fear. This is due to unreleased experiences with them, unfinished business, or karmic contracts. Many of you have been mistreated in other existences by these people, and so you feel fear or concern when you see them. The presence of these entities brings to your consciousness hidden memories that lie alive in your subconscious minds.

- **Genetic inheritance (negative factors)...**Sacred Code 314

  - **Identify repressed subconscious material that prevents the manifestation...**Sacred Code 819. By means of this code they will be able to identify this material and cancel its effects.

- **Release from Karmic Contracts...**Sacred Code 288 and 1118

- **Get rid of the actions of disincarnate karmic enemies...**Sacred Code 323

- **The lords of karma...**Sacred Code 95138

- **Protection against karmic revenge...**Sacred Code 212. There are several people who want revenge on many of you for karmic reasons, if they have not already done so. Make use of the code sothat you are not caught off guard.

- **To give Light and relief to your Loved Ones...**Sacred Code 025

- **People who were not wanted by their parents...**Sacred Code 224. So that they obtain their healing.

- **Receive everything that their parents could not give them while they were incarnated...** Sacred Code 18000. This Code is ge-nial, because it allows Parents from the Unity of the Spirit, to pour out a torrent of blessings on those who were their children in this incarnation. When I speak of blessings, they are helps of all kinds, including material needs. The Parents of these Souls yearn with all their strength to be able to act on their children, since there are no longer contracts that limit them, and the love that they can offer them is overflowing, without borders.

- **Painful Memories During the 9 Months of Stay in the Maternal Womb (sa-nar)...**Sacred Code 52

- **-Harrowing Memories from 9 Months to 7 Years Old (sa-nar)...**Sacred Code 919

- **Negative Memories from 7 Years to 18 Years (heal)**...Sacred Code 59

- **Recover lost time**...Sacred Code 822. You are going to reap the harvest of your efforts of so many years.

- **Regressions to the near and remote past ...** Sacred Code 427. We can enter a hypnotic trance and ask Archangel Raziel to be our Guide in these regressions.

- **Know what the next step is ...**Sacred Code 114. By means of this code it will be clearly revealed to uswhat is the next step we must take. This is excellent,because in advance we will know in which stage we are going to move.

- **Bringing up repressed material from other lives ...**Sacred Code 442

- **Disembodied loved ones ...** Sacred Code 21315. Think of the disincarnated Loved One that you have loved the most in this life. Through this Code, he will return to assist you and be by your side in this last stretch. Even if you don't see him, he will be your greatest help. Listen to him, because he will speak to you, comfort you and tell you what you have to do at every moment.

- **Live in the present moment ...**Sacred Code 789. We must never lose hope because God can change our luck in a fraction of a second. The Universe may arrive at the last minute, but it always arrives on time. Living the Present is the key. We usually have a tendency to be in the past or in the future. Through this Code we will anchor ourselves in the moment, abandoning our heads, and immersing ourselves in the world of the senses.

Increase our capacity to demonstrate

- **Angel Tetragramatron ...**Sacred Code 28720. Activate your Body of Light, and open yourability to manifest.

- **Angel Nascela ...**Sacred Code 62174. It helps all those who have their creativity blocked and cannot visualize adequately. It offers an invaluable aid in the rapid development of talents.

- **The 7 angels who rule the law of attraction** ...Sacred Code 87949. You will attract the special graces of These 7 Spirits, they will greatly facilitate your power of manifestation, so that you can achieveyour objectives. The quota that you will offer is the intention to remain positive.) The Angels are: Imael,Orael, Saniel, Urael, Minael, Somael and Arsiel.

- **Spiritual Mentoring Program: Neville**

  Goddard (1905-1972) ... Sacred Code 61571. Neville can help us visualize successfully. He was a Master on this subject. Most people have their visualization power blocked, making it difficult for them to construct mental images.

  We must be certain that if we work with Neville, he will help us and listen.

Holistic therapies help

- **Activate automatic writing...** Sacred Code 6726

- **Channeling (facilitate)...**Sacred Code 499

- **Clairaudience (magnify)...**Sacred Code 777

- **Clairvoyance (develop)...**Sacred Code 70225, 2315 and 1618

- **Development of Telepathy...**Sacred Code 19813

- **Develop medium skills...**Sacred Code 58829

- **Desire to be Healed...**Sacred Code 111500. It is used in people who consider a disease to bring benefits and block any help consciously or unconsciously.

- **Natural gifts (Ruth of Andromeda)...**Sacred code 49816

- **Prime...**Sacred Code 3366. Whoever wants to develop Clairaudience and Clairvoyance, quickly use the mandaic form called The Flower Of Life. Look carefully at that figure, as if wanting to immerse yourself in its vibratory field, and the aforementioned faculties will open to you. Those who workin the field of Ra-diestesia, do your readings bear-ing below the pendulum the flower of life. Withouta doubt, your diagnoses will be more accurate.

- **Interpret unfamiliar scripts, symbols, and languages ...**Sacred Code 19996

- **Laying on of hands (potential effects of the) ...**Sacred Code 1515

- **Intuition...**Sacred Code 811

- **Miracles...**Sacred Code 4418 and 1913. Offered by Merlin to obtain miracles.

- **To favor the interpretation of the Tarot...** Sacred Code 1133

- **For Conscious Astral Travel...** Sacred Code 729

- **Distant Healing Thought (Important)...** Sacred Code 580

- **Psychometry...**Sacred Code 251212. They will learn to capture the energy of people, places andobjects.

- **Enhance Reiki...**Sacred Code 1515

- **Dowsing (getting correct answers) ...**
- Sacred Code 579

- **Akashic Records (enter) ...**Sacred Code 9871

- **Conscious breathing ...**Sacred Code 2500. This single action will anchor you in the present, it will connect permanently with us.

- **Distance Healing ...**Sacred Code 110834

- **Telekinesis...**Sacred Code 680

- **Merkaba Vehicle (activate) ...**Sacred Code 360

Farms

- **Angels of the chakras** ...Sacred Code 996

- Sky star chakra Sacred Code 56 (on the head, etheric body).

- **Farm 1** ...Sacred Code 760

- **Farm 2** ...Sacred Code 451

- **Farm 3** ...Sacred Code 293

- **Farm 4** ...Sacred Code 741

- **Farm 5** ...Sacred Code 986

- **Farm 6** ...Sacred Code 505

- **Farm 7** ...Sacred Code 204

- **Earth star chakra** ...Sacred Code 264 (underfoot, internal on earth).

Life and death

- **Shorten the time spent on the Plan ...** Sacred Code 72718. Whoever uses this number, by a special grace, will have their life on the planet shortened. There are souls who wish to leave, with this number they will reduce their time here.

- **Angel of life ...**Sacred Code 887

  - **Assigning souls from purgatory to help** ...Sacred Code 44197: Each person is assigned 3 "Souls from Purgatory". As is known, these Souls left unfinished business in their last incarnation, and so to speak there was a delay in their advance. This situation has them stagnant in what are called "Purga-torial Lakes". By Law of Attraction, these Souls can help us, because the issues that they left pending are the same that each one of us has pending. Logically receiving the 3 Souls is not mandatory. It is only for those who want to use them.

- **Grief and losses...**Sacred Code 1962

- **Death date...**Sacred Code 62116. To whoever uses this Number, the date of his "death" will be revealed. In reality, death does not exist, which means that you will be clearly told when you are going to disincarnate.

- **Get a quiet death...** Sacred Code 6215
- **Inner peace...**Sacred Code 1. Help someone who is dying.

  - **To handle grief and the loss of a loved one** ...Sacred Code 1962

- **Ask for souls in purgatory ...** Sacred Code 44197

- **People who have committed suicide ...** Sacred Code 72952

- **Receive everything that their parents could not give them while they were incarnated...** Sacred Code 18000. This Code is genial, because it allows Parents from the Unity of the Spirit, to pour out a torrent of blessings on those who were their children in this incarnation. When I speak of blessings, they are helps of all kinds, including material needs. The Parents of these Souls yearn with all their strength to be able to act on their children, since there are no longer contracts that limit them, and the love that they can offer them is overflowing, without borders.

- **Know if a person is alive or deceased...**Sacred Code 33020

- **Disembodied beings ...**Sacred Code 100

- **Disembodied loved ones...** Sacred Code 21315 and 718. You will feel like never before the presence and help of your disembodied loved ones, who will guide you even in the smallest details of daily life andwill give you signs.

Computers

- **Computers**...Sacred Code 1900. (Use this Code before starting to work on your computers, you will be free from electromagnetic pollution and invisible harmful energies).

- **Computers (In Case of Strange Failures**...Sa- cred Code 052. It can also be used in other devices.

- **Computers (Failed to connect, No connection)**... Sacred Code 177

Heal Animals General

- **Abandoned animals (Attraction of Tu-tores for adoption)...**Sacred Code 2008 and 3050.

- **Animals (immunity to disease)...**Sacred Code 313. This assumes on the part of the owner of the animal, optimal environmental conditions and correct hygiene.

- **Animals (protection against low energy)...**Sacred Code 415

- **Attraction of Animal Mentors...**Sacred Code 2008

- **Animal Protection...**Sacred Code 52798

Cats

- **Anemia...**Sacred Code F-145

- **Kidney stones ...**Sacred Code 6931

- **Cancer...**Sacred Code L-120

- **Cataracts in cats ...**Sacred Code 3120

- **Cystitis...**Sacred Code 21400

- **Connection with the Soul of cats...**Sacred Code 66925

- **Pain...**Sacred Code 157-X

- **Joint pain in cats ...**Sacred Code 1613

- **Lack of appetite in cats ...**Sacred Code 1571

- **Swollen glands in cats ...**Sacred Code 881

- **Gingivitis in the mouth of cats ...**Sacred Code 5527

- **Liver...**Sacred Code 721-M
- **Heart failure in cats ...** Sacred Code 6060

- **Leukemia...**Sacred Code X-420

- **Stomach nodules ...**Sacred Code 2531-X

- **Esophageal nodules ...**Sacred Code 827-X

- **Ulcers in the mouth of cats ...**Sacred Code 88821

Dogs

- **Anemia in dogs ...**Sacred Code 801

- **Hips for age ...** Sacred Code F-715

- **Cancer in dogs ...**Sacred Code 2412

- **Calm aggressive dogs ...**Sacred Code 282

- **Cataracts in dogs ...**Sacred Code 6053

- **Cystitis in dogs ...**Sacred Code 1190

- **Joint pain in dogs ...**Sacred Code 1181

- **Pulmonary emphysema ...**Sacred Code F-306

- **Epilepsy and seizures ...**Sacred Code F-744

- **Ticks ...**Sacred Code 1639

- **Hemorrhoids in Dogs ...**Sacred Code F-231

- **Mushrooms...**Sacred Code 102

- **Liver in dogs** ...Sacred Code F-728

- **Heart failure in dogs** ... Sacred Code 1218

- **Canine distemper** ...Sacred Code 670

- **Paralysis in dogs** ...Sacred Code F-180

- **Parvovirus in dogs** ...Sacred Code F-214
- **Spinal problems in dogs** ...Sacred Code 618

- **Fleas on animals** ...Sacred Code1520

- **Rheumatism**...Sacred Code T-729

- **Kidneys in dogs** ...Sacred Code 539

- **Scabies in dogs** ...Sacred Code 0517

Power animals

- **Bees ...**Sacred Code 861

- **Eagle...**Sacred Code 179

- **Armadillo...**Sacred Code 729

- **Buffalo...**Sacred Code 821

- **Owl...**Sacred Code 21

- **White owl...**Sacred Code 01. Here I speak of the Owl as Power Animal. Whoever uses this Number will feel the tremendous protection of the White Owland its ability to override the plans of third parties who want to harm you in some way.

- **Horse...**Sacred Code 315

- **Zebra as a Totem or Power Animal ...**Sacred Code 384

- **Kangaroo...**Sacred Code 159

- **Silver Cobra ...**Sacred Code 616

- **Hummingbird ...**Sacred Code 620

- **Dolphins ...**Sacred Code 701

- **Dragon...**Sacred Code 020

- **Elephant...**Sacred Code 21

- **Cat...**Sacred Code 94

- **Cricket as Power Animal ...**Sacred Code 734
- **Hawk...**Sacred Code 30

- **Ant...**Sacred Code 28

- **Giraffe...**Sacred Code 374

- **Lion...**Sacred Code 89

- **Leopard...**Sacred Code 757

- **White Wolf...**Sacred Code 664

- **Chuck ...**Sacred Code 515

- **Butterfly...**Sacred Code 33

- **Blackbird...**Sacred Code 526

- **Birds** ...Sacred Code 52114

- **Black Panther...**Sacred Code 524 and 789

- **Fish...**Sacred Code 2120

- **Pegasus...**Sacred Code 100100 and 00315

- **Dog...**Sacred Code 61

- **Rhinoceros...**Sacred Code 424

- **Snake...**Sacred Code 615

- **Tiger...**Sacred Code 596

- **White Tiger...**Sacred Code 681

- **Turtles** ...Sacred Code 089

- **Unicorn...**Sacred Code 7 and 14147

Countries, Continents and Oceans

- **Angels Powers ...**Sacred Code 70-27. There is an Army of Angels called Powers, which you can turn to to change the world situation, and believe me they are effective and miraculous.

- **Colombia...**Sacred Code 01

- **Venezuela...**Sacred Code 02

- **Argentina...**Sacred Code 03

- **Chili...**Sacred Code 04

- **Peru...**Sacred Code 05

- **Mexico...**Sacred Code 06

- **Japan...**Sacred Code 07

- **Panama...**Sacred Code 09

- **Costa Rica...**Sacred Code 011

- **Ecuador...**Sacred Code 012

- **Bolivia** ...Sacred Code 013

- **Uruguay**...Sacred Code 014

- **Paraguay** ...Sacred Code 015

- **Brazil**...Sacred Code 016

- **Australia**...Sacred Code 017

- **France**...Sacred Code 019

- **U.S**...Sacred Code 020
- **Cuba**...Sacred Code 022

- **Poland**...Sacred Code 023

- **Syria**...Sacred Code 028

- **Europe**...Sacred Code 620

- **Asia**...Sacred Code 30

- **Africa**...Sacred Code 94

- **America**...Sacred Code 45

- **Oceania...**Sacred Code 116

- **Pacific Ocean...**Sacred Code 200 • Atlantic Ocean ... Sacred Code 250

- **Indian Ocean...**Sacred Code 300

- **Antartic Ocean...**Sacred Code 350

- **Arctic Ocean...**Sacred Code 400

The planet earth and its environment

- **Food and water** ...Sacred Code 091

- **Angel of the Earth** ...Sacred Code 331

- **Support mother earth** ...Sacred Code 88845. If each Soul from his home and at the time he chooses, repeats this Sacred Code, it would mobilize a powerful energy of solidarity that would avoid many setbacks and would favor the Planet.

- **Connect with the earth**...Sacred Code 625

- **Establish a connection with Mother Earth**...Sacred Code 222

- **Precipitate rain**...Sacred Code 112258. In places where there are great droughts. Its effect is enhanced if the Angels of the weather are called.

- **For the sun to rise**...Sacred Code 465. This Code is used when there are prolonged rains.

- **Garbage in the waters**...Sacred Code 929
  Codes for the health of The Kingdoms:
- **Animal**...Sacred Code 290

- **Vegetable...**Sacred Code 316

- **Mineral...**Sacred Code 720

- **Environmental pollution...**Sacred Code 25450

- **Weed and pest control ...**Sacred Code 379, 434, and 643

- **Oil spill...**Sacred Code 818

- **Soil decontamination and PH balance.**Sacred Code 15027

- **Decontamination of Lagos ...**Sacred Code 52127

- **Decontamination of Rivers ...**Sacred Code 82030

- **Decontamination of Seas ...**Sacred Code 7521

- **Pond Decontamination ...** Sacred Code 82031

- **To help Animals that "die" in fires and natural disasters ...**Sacred Code 4418

- **Control of worms in plantations ...**Sacred

Code 1412

- **Produce a benefit to any Plantor Sown**
  ...Sacred Code 1616. It is as if we paid it.

- **Angel Carona** ...Sacred Code 52137. This Angel-gel teaches you to protect yourself in case of storms and tempests.

- **Angel Raaschiel** ...Sacred Code 65. It is used in case of earthquakes.

- **Weather Angels** ...Sacred Code 757, 758 and 759

- **Angels of natural phenomena** ... Sacred Code 775

- **Increase size in fruits and vegetables** ... Sacred Code 069

- **Inside plants**...Sacred Code 1901

- **Garden plants**...Sacred Code 2114

- **Tree**...Sacred Code 620

- **Birds (Woodpecker)**...Sacred Code 3070

- **Milky cows**...Sacred Code 10069

- **Moss Agate**...Sacred Code 526

- **Amethyst**...Sacred Code 52318

- **Angelita**...Sacred Code 75334

- **Citrine**...Sacred Code 8814

- **Cornelian**...Sacred Code 2190

- **Quartz Crystal**...Sacred Code 219

- **Rose Quartz**...Sacred Code 1718

- **Jade**...Sacred Code 1527

- **Red Jasper** ...Sacred Code 111334

- **Lapiz Lazuli**...Sacred Code 52277

- **Black Obsidian**...Sacred Code 8228

- **Peridot**...Sacred Code 216

- **Gem Bull's Eye**...Sacred Code 2715

- **Onyx...**Sacred Code 715
- **Black Tourmaline...**Sacred Code 7777777
- **The reprogramming of genetically treated seeds ...**Sacred Code 191329

- **Chemtrails and Haarp ...**Sacred Code 457

- **To positively enlighten the Rulers ...**Sacred Code 4972

Planets of origin

- **Mother Mary in her invocation of Our Lady of The Miraculous Medal ...**Code Sa-degree 27 or 927. Through these Codes, a wisdom that is not of the earth will be transmitted to you, so that you can apply it in your day to day life. Those who do not yet know which planet they belong to, make the request of me, and I will enlighten them.

- **Ageon ...**Sacred Code 001

- **Sirius...**Sacred Code 002

- **Pleiades ...**Sacred Code 003

- **Andromeda...**Sacred Code 004

- **Orion...**Sacred Code 005

- **Mars...**Sacred Code 006

- **Arcturus ...**Sacred Code 007

- **Venus...**Sacred Code 008

- **Purple...**Sacred Code 009

- **Oasibeth ...**Sacred Code 0010

- **Alpha Centaur Star System ...**Sacred Code 0011

- **Earth...**Sacred Code 0014

Solar system

- **Connection with the Sun ...**Sacred Code 1

- **Moon...**Sacred Code 547

- **Connection with the Moon ...**Sacred Code 2

Beings of the DivineRealm

The source (The father creator of all)

- **The fountain...**Sacred Code 111 and 883. It is revealed through The Inner Voice

- **Golden white ray of the Divine Father...**Sacred Codes 1111

  - **Platinum silver ray of the Divine Mother...** Sacred Code 3333

- **Beloved Presence I Am...**Sacred Code 636 and 464. The Presence that introduces you to that world you always dreamed of, I am the end of suffering and the fulfillment of your heart's desires.

- **Higher self...**Sacred Code 864

Jesus and his invocations

- **Jesus...**Sacred Code 41933. Jesus, like Mother Mary, has a general Code, but uses other Codes in their invocations or aspects.

- **Blood of Christ...**Sacred Code 111

- **Wounds (Wounds) of Christ...**Sacred Code 950

- **Holy Trinity...**Sacred Code 4972

- **Childhood of Jesus (receive thanks)...**Sacred Code 144

- **Child Jesus...**Sacred Code 144. For desperate situations and to apply it to children.

- **Infant Jesus of Atocha...**Sacred Code 701

- **Infant Jesus of Prague...**Sacred Code 689, 2733 and 1189

- **Divine mercy...**Sacred Code 7 and 2033

- **Extension of divine mercy...**Sacred Code 18

- **Dulcify great sorrows...**Sacred Code 515This Number springs from the greatest love of the Holy Spirit. It is to soften great sorrows, to console the Souls who suffer for whatever reason. Whoever uses it will feel that he is comforted in the most inti-mate of his being.

- **Immunity Against Any Illness...** Sacred Code 72249. As the most close followers of the Master Jesus.

- **Lord of Luren (Peru)...**Sacred Code 2820

- **Lady Nada (Mary Magdalene)...** Sacred Code 771. Goddess of transfiguration.

- **Judas Thaddeus...**Sacred Code 16700 and 45600.It can be called in the following cases or situations: Abuse, Despair, Consolation, Successful negotia- tions, Real knowledge of Jesus.

- **Juan...**Sacred Code 334 and 425. Health and prosperity, Attacks against physical integrity, help those who channel, Liberation from dangers, Knowledge of Mother Mary.

- **Santiago the eldest...**Sacred Code 16699. Pro-tection of the 5 physical senses, Development of the power of the spoken word, Helps those who work in the field of Dowsing, Accompanies them on trips.

- **Santiago the less...**Sacred Code 16701. Grant peace around, Get good friends, Help to do justice, Achieve success and skill in prayers.

- **Philip...**Sacred Code 826. Helps men find a life partner and women a life partner, Improves human relationships, Attracts healers and healing methods.

- **Bartholomew...**Sacred Code 576. Helps to shed the "old energy", Free from "false beliefs", Helps to find healthy and good vibes places to feed.

- **Peter...**Sacred Code 591. Gives protection, Increases faith.

- **Simon ...**Sacred Code 661. Get good relationships with neighbors, Provide a peaceful and restful sleep, Help people with skin problems.

- **You take ...** Sacred Code 15573. Free from decep-tions and traps, Attracts Divine Mercy.

- **Andrew...**Sacred Code 8914. Helps improve family relationships, Improve mental health by teaching people to have fun.

- **Matthew...**Sacred Code 212. Get Mentors in

financ-es, Teach the correct handling of money, Help in everything related to Computer Science.

- **Matías** ...Sacred Code 21513. Gives hope, Gives calm to whoever requests it.
- **Sarah (daughter of Jesus)**...Sacred Code 61124. I am one of the purest expressions of Divine Love, I was chosen to appear at this time. I have come so that you, especially those who do not feel loved, perceive love at all levels.

- **Jaime (Brother of Jesus)**...Sacred Code 68114

- **Martha (friend of Jesus, sister of Láza-ro)** ...Sacred Code 527. It gives the gift of faith, the ability to dare, to take risks

- **Legrashogua**...Sacred Code 1596. One of the teachers of Jesus the Christ.
- **Holy Grail**...Sacred Code 114. You will connect with the energy of the holy grail and will know the true story of Jesus the Christ and his closest ser-vants. The aforementioned Code will also allow them to experience a very close relationship with the Master Jesus, and receive his infinite bless-ings. They will also know who Maria Magdalena was and is, and the role she plays with The As-cended Souls.

Mother Mary and her invocations

- **Childhood of Mother Mary...**Sacred Code 521. Through this number you can get special and unique gifts from Her.

- **Virgin of Peace...**Sacred Code 1710

- **Mother Mary...**Sacred Code 333. Mother of Jesus, Cosmic Mother. Patron of Healing

- **Mother Mary...**Sacred Code 212019. Whoever uses this Number will reveal useful and important secrets.

- **Angels escorting Mother Mary...**Sacred Code 5533

- **Mother Mary in her invocation of our lady of Caacupe...**Sacred Code 52190

- **Mother Mary in her invocation of Our Lady of Carmen...**Sacred Code 1516

- **Mother Mary in her invocation of the Immaculate Conception...**Sacred Code 2614

- **Mother Mary in her invocation as Our Lady of Consolation...**Sacred Code 12573.

Mother Mary in her invocation of our lady of Coromoto... Sacred Code 1615

- **Mother Mary in her Advocation (Divina Pastora)...**Sacred Code 2070

- **Mother Mary in her invocation of our Lady of Sorrows...**Sacred Code 58721

- **Mother Mary in her invocation of Our Lady of Guadalupe...**Sacred Code 12

- **Mother Mary in her invocation of our lady of Loreto...**Sacred Code 373 and 1211

- **Mother Mary in her invocation of Our Lady of the Miraculous Medal...**Code Sa-degree 27 or 927.

- **Mother Mary in her invocation of Mary Au-xiliadora...**Sacred Code 115

- **Mother Mary in her Advocation (La Candelaria)...**Sacred Code 63

- **Mother Mary in her invocation of our lady of Lourdes...**Sacred Code 1201

- **Mother Mary in her invocation of Our Lady of Lourdes...**Sacred Code 721. This Code is for working with chronic diseases.
- **Mother Mary in her invocation of our lady of Las Mercedes...**Sacred Code 13000. We can invoke it today and always with this number.

- **Mother Mary in her Aspect or Advocation of Our Lady of Monserrat...**Sacred Code 32010

- **Mother Mary in her invocation of Our Lady of the Rosary...**Sacred Code 7611. This Code provides spectacular protectionagainst accidents.
- **Mother Mary in her invocation of Our Lady of the Sacred Heart...**Sacred Code 844.

- **Mother Mary in her invocation of Our Lady of Urkupiña...**Sacred Code 559

- **Dream state...**Sacred Code 27. Mother Mary: It is optimal in two moments: in the morning, when they are still in their beds, becoming aware of awakening, they are neither asleep nor awake; This is where you must repeat my Code mentally or as a whisper. Returning to the idea, there is a moment in the morning when they are neither asleep nor awake, they are about to wake up and open their eyes. This is where they must repeat the Code. Daydreaming if you will is a hypnotic state where your subconscious obeys you and is highly receptive. In the morning (is what I just explained), and at night. There is a moment when you are ready to rest, when you are about to fall asleep; They are not yet asleep, nor are they awake. In that intermediate state you must recite my Code as a whisper or in your mind. What is the wonderful thing about this My Loves? that throughout the night the Code will be working for you. As you fall asleep, your last thought is the Sacred Code. This is great because they can change quickly and visibly. In time, they will wake up fresh and cheerful, full of vitality.

They will sleep more peacefully and see remarkable changes in their lives.

Saints

- **Saint Augustine of Hippo...**Sacred Code 100

- **Saint Anthony of padua...**Sacred Code 858 (It is the recuperator of lost assets).

- **San Benito...**Sacred Code 26123

- **San Cayetano...**Sacred Code 817. It will guarantee your material and spiritual sustenance.

- **Saint Catherine of Bologna...**Sacred Code 26700

- **San Ceferino Namancura...**Sacred Code 1615

- **Saint Charbel...**Sacred Code 799

- **San Cristobal...**Sacred Code 918

- **Saint Cone...**Sacred Code 199

- **Holy Army of Hidden Saints...**Sacred Code 654

- **San expedito**...Sacred Code 454545 or 92. San Expedito attends to our most urgent cases that need an immediate resolution and that due to theirdelay would cause great damage.

- **Saint Philomena**...Sacred Code 127, 59942, and 1998. The power it has and the wonders it works is so great that it has three Codes. It is also beautiful.

- **San Francisco de Asis**...Sacred Code 521

- **San Francisco Solano** ...Sacred Code 1570

- **Gem Galgani** ...Sacred Code 665

- **Saint Hildegarde of Bingen** ...Sacred Code 1679

- **Saint Ignatius of Loyola** ...Sacred Code 614

- **Saint Jude Thaddeus** ...Sacred Code 16700 or 45600. With the certainty of receiving prompt and visible help. Each one ask your Soul to take you tonight to the Etheric Retreat of this Great Being, located in the Region of Armenia (Russia). Do not miss this unique opportunity. Judas Thaddeus helps in the most serious tribulations and has the power to make wonders).

- **Santa Laura Montoya** ...Sacred Code 445

- **Saint Lazarus (brother of Martha, the friend of Jesus) ...**Sacred Code 528.

- **St. Lucia...**Sacred Code 98

- **Santa Maria de la Rabida ...**Sacred Code 1122

- **San Martin de Porres...**Sacred Code 994. This Soul is prodigious. The dying dark entities have tried to damage healings done by Archangel Raphael, and this wonderful being has prevented them. I recommend visiting their Etheric Retreat. Whoever does it will not come out empty-handed.

- **San Pancracio ...**Sacred Code 1670

- **St. Patrick...**Sacred Code 39

- **San Ramón Nonato ...**Sacred Code 424. It helps us not to walk again on inconvenient routes in which on some occasion we have already experienced without success.

- **Santa Rita...**Sacred Code 52550

- **San Roque...**Sacred Code 556. For any contagious disease, This Being of Light is very faithful and compassionate.

- **Saint Thérèse of Lisieux ...**Sacred Code 2 and 2020. Whoever wants to fly high and fast, seek the protection of my Beloved Daughter Teresita de Lisieux, she is an expert in speed. She has said that she wants to spend her Heaven doing good to Earth, and the Roses are her Symbol. She has communicated to me that her Code can be used forall kinds of situations. He suggests to himself that while we are repeating the Code, we visualize Ros- es in the affected organ or situation to be treated. Iinsist that your Code is for everything we can thinkof.

- **Teresita de Lisieux ...**Sacred Code 04. When you feel that a decision is going to be made in which you will be harmed. It is a special number that she grants us for specific cases.

Angelic Kingdom

- **Seraphim...**Sacred Code 211. These Beings can be called upon in case of earthquakes, accidents, or any type of natural disaster. They can bring much relief to people who suffer from these calamities. Any of us can call them on the Number quoted, and they will go where we send them.

- **Cherubs...**Sacred Code 315. They are very helpful in cases of exhaustion and fatigue. This circumstance makes people easily prey to anguish. Cherubs can restore peace of mind and harmony.

- **Thrones...**Sacred Code 809. They can help us find good friends and solve problems with people. They heal painful memories caused by troubled relationships.

- **Dominations...**Sacred Code 2510. These Angels are experts in helping us to listen to the heart, and in distinguishing the voices that hover in the mind.

- **Virtues...**Sacred Code 901. They are in charge of the healing of the earth. We can send them to the places that man destroys, especially those related to nature. Any work we do in this regard will do.

- **Powers...**Sacred Code 457. Its function is to eliminate negativity, bad vibrations, combat against the "dark" forces. To this choir belongs Kinaya Sakwa of Ageón.

- **Principalities...**Sacred Code 670. They are in charge of the urban part. We can ask them for specific help for where we live, even for our neighborhood.

- **Archangels:** I have already talked about them in detail, They are many. There are currently 999 on the planet, and they are in charge of making Divine Justice shine.

- **Angels....**Sacred Code 294. Here are the Guardian Angels, and the millions of Angels who daily work for all Human Beings. We can give them specific tasks.

Angels

- **7 Angels of Violet Fire...**Sacred Code 5293. Archangel Zadquiel has offered to send them, to whoever requests them.

- **Angels...**Sacred Code 44. To attract help and get rid of lower entities that try to stick to our aura.

- **Angel Abel...**Sacred Code 784. A white angel from the Syrian planet. The one who offers you a different and beautiful panorama, the one who is willing to create a miraculous solution for you.

- **Angel of abundance (Abundia)...**Sacred Code 71269. This Angel is loving and rescues Souls from poverty. He gives us messages in dreams and takes care of what we have of value.

- **Angels of plenty...**Sacred Code 1929. Numerous Group of Angels. They are waiting for your orders to go into action.

- **Angels of plenty...**Sacred Code is 4972. We are the messengers of the Flame of the sun, a bridge between the Divine and the earthly.

- **Accelerating angels...**Sacred Code 2080. The Soul has a plan, and if it cannot carry it out, it harms its evolutionary process. These Angels freethe Soul from ruin, and remove karmic, personaland cosmic obstacles. Whoever invokes these be-ings will notice that a great weight is lifted from their shoulders, they will feel freedom, ease, and will see that God and the universe are on your side, not against you.

- **Angel Afrei …**Sacred Code 3720. It is one of those beings that, upon reaching our life, fills it with magic and beautiful things.

- **Angel Anichiel …**Sacred Code 844. This Angel-gel is a defense against the attacks of your karmic enemies who already glimpsed your defeat.

- **Angel Adonaiel …**Sacred Code 32511 and 727. Take an Exam

- **Angel Alagill …**Sacred Code 52511. This Angel gives us total success at work

- **Angel Amiel …**Sacred Code 339

- **Angel Anephaxetón …**Sacred Code 1913. Help to manage your merkaba and manifest your desires, along with the angels primeumaton and tetra-grammaton.

  - **The Arelim (Warrior Angels of white fire)**

...Sacred Code 614. The most powerful squad of the Heavenly Army of Archangel Michael.

- **Angel Areniel** ...Sacred Code 411. This Angel is an advisor in the field of accounts and numbers. You can ask for help when you need to keep some accounting, or you want some fluency and familiarity with mathematics.

- **Angels of the most extreme and delicate com- passion**...Sacred Code 78631. They will make them company at the very moment they pronounce theircode.

- **Angels governing the Law of Attraction...** Sacred Code 87949. Imael, Orael, Saniel, Urael, Minael, Somael, Arsiel. To attract special thanks; They will facilitate their power of manifestation. The share stay positive.

- **Angels Amelee**...Sacred Code 8887. These Angels can be invoked in cases of intense fear and hopelessness.

- **Angel Love**...Sacred Code 70-27. Feel my closeness and enjoy my energy, I am LOVE, a feminine Angel of sweetness, an energy that is not governed by human laws.

- **Angel Anauel**...Sacred Code 379. He is the

Angelof business and businessmen.

- **Alsemiyat...**Sacred Code 72599. Commander of the warriors of fire, this Angel relieves people who are oppressed and suffer for any cause. He who frees them from the spirits of ruin and misery, and breaks the chains that oppress them.
- **Angel Asinel...**Sacred Code 53728. It governs happiness and whoever makes a connection with it will perceive its beneficial influence. It reveals the secrets of faith, and teaches us to discover hidden enemies.

- **Angel Astriel...**Sacred Code 2430. It is one of the greatest helps against disincarnated karmic enemies. A Being of Light specialized in this Field and whose Sacred Code is him.

- **Angel Aurora...**Sacred Code 774 So that you keep those lights on, and your life changes significantly.

- **Angel Bagoloni...**Sacred Code 2194. Send telepathy, transmission of thought at this time.

- **Angel Barachel...**Sacred Code 311. Help with legal problems.

- **Angel Bath Kol...**Sacred Code 62030. The one that invites them to put into practice what they have learned, the one that teaches them to discover miracles.

- **Angels of Well-being ...**Sacred Code 607

- **White angels of the Syrian planet...**Sacred Code 559. You can also attract our vibration through Psalm 91.

- **Angel Cambriel...**Sacred Code 286. Angel of the Month of January

- **Angel Barchiel...**Sacred Code 69. Angel of the Month of February

- **Angel Carona...**Sacred Code 52137. It teaches them to protect themselves from storms and tempests.

- **Angel Cerviel...**Sacred Code 489. The Guardian Angel of King David, the one who with my powerful help defeated the giant Goliath.

- **Angel Colopatirón...**Sacred Code 615. This Angel bestows the gift of independence. To be independent is to be free. Whoever depends on someone cannot be "the same".

- **Angel Cumael ...**Sacred Code 1122

- **Angel Danijel ...**Sacred Code 62515. Angel of divine justice. Go to him if you feel unfairly treated in any area.

- **Weather Angels ...**Sacred Code 757

- **Angels of the day ...**Sacred Code 55

- **The Angels of the Phoenix Bird Nebula ...**Sacred Code 0447. They are defenders par excellence, Protective and invincible Warriors. **Angel of the Restoration...**Sacred Code 1

- **Angel of the last hour...**Sacred Code 1777. The energies that descended on August 23, resolved many agreements of wills that you had with other entities, not only from this one, but from other lives. The people with whom they had the aforementioned agreements, may disappear from their lives, or they will start a new and different relationship with them based on the new energy. So be on the lookout, and you will find out what will happen.

- **Golden Angels...**Sacred Code 744. Babaji has said that these angels solve extreme situations, heal the wounds that prevent the advent of prosperity.

- **Golden Angel Augustine...**Sacred Code 335 connect with my energy.

- **Angel Elyasim**...Sacred Code 123 and 215. The An-gel that reveals secrets and opens unknown doors. Heis one of the Guardians of Our Heart. The heart is un-known to us, and this Angel makes it known to us.

- **The guardian angels of the divine mercy**... Sacred Code 7160. If you invoke them, you will receive many favors.

- **Fire Warrior Squad**...Sacred Code 82977. Powerful angels to subdue the dark forces.
- **The Angels of the Holy Spirit**... Sacred Code 16158887

- **Angels of Natural Phenomena**...Sacred Code 775

- **Florián's Angels**...Sacred Code 1615

- **Guardian Angels**...Sacred Code 525

These angels belong to the Belt Zone of the Earth and are, if you will, the telephones to communicate with other Dimensions:

- **Angel Granona**...Sacred Code 12179

- **The Angels of Mother Mary...**Sacred Code 901. There are very sensitive Souls who suffer a lot in these events, and they tend to see the future with despair. To counteract these feelings, go to them.

- **Angel Mennolika...**Sacred Code 02412

- **Angel Hanael...**Sacred Code 23715. The Angel of the Month of December His Energy is closely related to The Goddess ISHTAR. This month is definitive in the Planetary Ascension process, hence Make it a priority to call Hanael whose main mission is to grant protection against darkness. This Angel comes as soon as he is invoked and quickly brings our requests to God.

- **Angel Inael...**Sacred Code 55511. Host of the angels of the one.

- **Angel Irín...**Sacred Code 1214. The one that consoles us in our sorrows.

- **Angel Jasel...**Sacred Code 8914

- **Angel Jasaiel of Mother Mary...**Sacred Code 1122. Telepathic Angel, a gift from the Lords of Karma.

- **Angel Jesael...**Sacred Code 728. Whoever invokes me will be sustained and I, in addition to helping him to believe, will increase his faith so that he can achieve his goals.

- **Angel Katzachiel...**Sacred Code 824. To surround yourself with silence, recollection.

- **Angel Kiliosa...**Sacred Code 7248. Helps in the most serious emergencies. This being is capable of rescuing people from their personal "chaos", if they ask for help.

- **Angel Maggid...**Sacred Code 711. An Angel of Justice who reveals secrets to you while you are in a hypnotic trance.

- **Angel Meher...**Sacred Code 72130. It is the Angel of compassion, and it helps all those who are going through difficult situations.
- **Angel Melekiel...**Sacred Code 65124. The angel of security

- **Angel Honey...**Sacred Code 254. This Angel greatly facilitates communication with us.

- **Angel Muriel...**Sacred Code 82010. Angel of the month of June.

- **Angel Negani...**Sacred Code 28500. It opens up immense possibilities

- **Angel Nascela...**Sacred Code 62174. It helps

anyone whose creativity is blocked and cannot visualize adequately, and it helps develop talents.

- **Night Angel...**Sacred Code 880

- **Angel Opilón** ...Sacred Code 294. This Angel is an ally to put circumstances in our favor.

- **Angel Orphiel...**Sacred Code 639. This Angel can be invoked in places where there is a lot of noise. He contributes to pacify the environment.

- **Pallas Angels...**Sacred Code 2639. These Angels are Masters in the art of Intuition. Whoever wants to develop this faculty already has someone to teach it to him.

- **Angel Parasiel...**Sacred Code 515. Prepare the way for abundance
- **Primeumaton Angel...**Sacred Code 443319. Helpto manage your merkaba and manifest your desire along with the angels Anaphaxeton and Tetragramatón.

- **Angel Raaschiel...**Sacred Code 65. It is used in case of earthquakes

- **Angel Redel...**Sacred Code 127. When you need wise advice, it will be revealed to you

- **Angel Remiel...**Sacred Code 21700. It helps us to anchor ourselves on the earth, and to connect with the body.

- **Angel Roel Haipar...**Sacred Code 72951

- **Angel of Wisdom...**Sacred Code 7000000. I makemy call to the 4 winds and whoever listens to me willhave the Holy Spirit of Wisdom, will see the glory of God, and will shine with my intense light. I invoke courage to those who sincerely invoke me.

- **Angels of the Seventh Heaven...**Sacred Code 8819618

- **Angel Samaral...**Sacred Code 7293

- **Angel Samandiriel...**Sacred Code 11921. The angel of imagination

- **Angel of Shambhala...**Sacred Code 14721. This Angel has an army of specialized servers in multiple areas. Every time you need his services, ask him to send a specialist Angel to where you need it. They will see how effective it is.

- **Angel Shateiel...**Sacred Code 12459. Angel of silence

- **Angels of Silence...**Sacred Code 777777

- **Angel Schaluach…**Sacred Code 2821

- **Angel Somi…**Sacred Code 88827. If you want secrets of the invisible world revealed, look for Somi.

- **Angel Tetragrammaton…**Sacred Code 28720. May your Body of Light activate, and open your ability to manifest.

- **Earth Angel…**Sacred Code 331

- **Angel Tmiti…**Sacred Code 28904. I am present in a time of great uncertainty for many of you. I am a Specialist in Divine Magic, and I am also the one who has transmitted all his magical knowledge to Mer-lín.

- **Angel of the Last Minute…**Sacred Code 1777. It helps to make plans so that we can achieve our goals, it makes us the path more bearable.
- **Angel Urirón…**Sacred Code 712754. It grants protection and liberation in cases of Sorcery (black magic). It also frees souls from sudden death.

- **See the Angels…**Sacred Code 120. With this Number, and the help of Saint Expedito, you will be able to see them.

- **Angel Victoria…**Sacred Code 151515 and 821

- **Angel of Life...**Sacred Code 887

- **Angel Wotariel...**Sacred Code 2190. It is a great relief for those who suffer, from any cause.

- **Angelic realm of the thirteenth dimension...**Sacred Code 14720. Every time you use this Code, the doors of the Fifth Dimension are opened to you, allowing you to attract lights and higher knowledge to be applied in your lives.

The Seven Main Archangels

- **Archangel Michael...**Sacred Code 613. Protection, Courage, Strength, Integrity, Truth. Sunday day.

- **Archangel Jofiel...**Sacred Code 521 and 431. Illumination, Wisdom, Creativity, Inspiration, Jubile. Monday.

- **Archangel Chamuel...**Sacred Code 725 and 125. Its gentle and powerful energy frees the captive Souls. Its Code is effective when couple, work, and family relationships are tense, Useful to those who are looking for their Soulmates and Kindred, to find their Divine mission, a job, or feel abandoned. Love, Empathy, Tenderness, Kindness, Understanding. Tuesday.

- **Archangel Gabriel....**Sacred Code 881 and 581. Guide, Purification, Vision, Expression, Mercy. Wednesday.

- **Invisibility Mantle of the Archangel Gabriel...**Sacred Code 882

- **Archangel Raphael...**Sacred Code 29,125, 2129 and 1577. Health, Transformation, Loyal- ty, Success, Leadership. Thursday. The one who presents our prayers to God so that he will take them into account.

- **Archangel Raphael's Personal Code...**Sacred Code 157. I recommend it to Healers, because if they practice it, they will become an extension of the Archangel. It is as if it transmits its healing qualities to the user of the Code.

- **Organ change...**Sacred Code 447. By means of this Code the Archangel Raphael can be asked for a change of organs. He can replace a damaged liver with a new one from his Organ Bank. The decision must be left to him. Sometimes this Archangel will heal a diseased organ by responding to someone who offers him various Codes. Other times, he decides, if he feels like it, that it is appropriate to change the organ for a new one, and he does it.

- **Archangel Uriel...**Sacred Code 4 and 411. Peace, Harmony, Devotion, Provision, Patience. Friday. It helps to materialize our dreams and to be successful in what we undertake.

- **Archangel Zadquiel...**Sacred Code 389. Liberation, Transmutation, Joy, Forgiveness, Acceptance. Saturday. It frees people from the inferiority complex and gives them Self-confidence.

The Seven Archangels

- **Arcangelina Esperanza...**Sacred Code 584. Divine complement of the Archangel Gabriel.

- **Arcangelina Maria...**Sacred Code 333. Divine complement of the Archangel Raphael.

- **Arcangelina Grace...**Sacred Code 996. Divine Complement of Archangel Uriel, the one that helps them to materialize their dreams.

- **Arcangelina Constanza...**Sacred Code 1891. Divine Complement of the Archangel Jofiel.

- **Archangel Amethyst...**Sacred Code 62114

- **Arcangelina Charity...**Sacred Code 28700

- **Arcangelina Fe...**Sacred Code 72128. His most intimate and reserved companion, the Divine Complement of Archangel Michael.

Other Archangels

- **Archangel Amalia**...Sacred Code 25701. One of the archangels of divine justice, divine complement of San Martín de Porres.

- **Archangel Ariel**...Sacred Code 29701

- **Archangel Azrael**...Sacred Code 17. He is anArangel who can help them when they have a loved one or friend who is about to disincarnate.

  Azrael helps him make contact with "the other Side" so that "death" is not traumatic. At the same time this Archangel is a great relief when a loved one has left.

  If someone in your family has passed away, calling Azrael is pretty good. It also helps to achieve communication with the loved ones who "have departed." In short, it is the Archangel to call in times of mourning.

- **Archangel Catherine**...Sacred Code 444444 and 169. One of the archangels of divine justice. Divine complement of san expedito.

- **Archangel Haniel**...Sacred Code 991. I will give you the strength to live out your talents. You are great and valuable. Bring before me those wishes that have not been fulfilled. What is difficult for you is not difficult for me. If you feel insecure and have lost confidence, come to me and you will come out refreshed. I offer you calm and joy.

- **Archangel Jeremiel...**Sacred Code 21700. The one that sharpens your intuition and gives you the key to clairvoyance.

- **Archangels of Divine Justice...**Sacred Code 999. The function of these Archangels is to carry out God's plan in the lives of those who embrace them.

- **Archangel Metatron...**Sacred Code 331

- **Archangel Natalia...**Sacred Code 553. Archangel-gel of divine justice. Divine Complement of San Judas Tadeo.

- **Archangel Nathaniel (Gift of God)...**Sacred Code 334. I am a specialist in making short-term changes, especially in relation to your life missions. Many are stuck, confused, living in toxic places with people who steal their energy, and without money to make profound changes. My name means GIFTFROM GOD, and I am the one who comes to help you change drastically and quickly. Maybe my way of acting and my energy shakes you, but it is time for you to put yourself in your true places and let your talents shine.

- They will gain the vigor and skill necessary to step

out of their comfort zone and face new horizons. For many this may seem frightening, as the unknown produces fear.

- **Archangel Paula...**Sacred Code 80427. One of the archangels of divine justice, Divine Complements of San Roque.

- **Archangel Raguel...**Sacred Codes 2129 and 136. Like Maat, Raguel embodies justice. I recommend that people who suffer some kind of abuse take refuge in it. Like Athena, is very skilled in conflict resolution, and teaches people to assert themselves. Grants bravery.

- **Archangel Raziel...**Sacred Code 679. It is very powerful and very wise. Imagine him as a grown man who has accumulated a lot of experience and knowledge. He knows all the secrets of the Universe and can help us a lot with his understanding to live a fuller life, in bliss and joy. His name means "secrets of God." His energy is masculine. Archangel Raziel helps us understand the secrets of the universe and teaches us esoteric knowledge such as the interpretation of dreams, among many other things. It is a very mystical Archangel-gel. Together with him you will learn a lot of spirituality and he will give you advice that will change your life, healing it from the roots.

- Within all his wisdom is helping us to remember and heal past lives. And it also helps us remove spiritual blocks. And finally, it helps us develop our psychic powers.

- **Archangel Sandalphon...**Sacred Code 820

Powers

- **Archangel Cassiel...**Sacred Code 781. He is the Prince of the Angels Powers and is part of the Seventh Heaven. To get what we want in the shortest time possible. Cassiel means SPEED GIFT OF GOD.

- **Angel Kinaya Sakwa...**Sacred Code 339716 or 99. (Female Angel) I belong to the Group of Angels called Powers and my home planet is Ageon. It has great power to subdue visible or invisible negative entities.

- **For Kinaya Sakwa to lower his power on a container of WATER...**Sacred Code 684. That we can use to drink or sprinkle it wherever we want.

- **Angels Powers...**Sacred Code 457. They are prodigious and can favorably alter the events of the world.

Seraphim

- **Justius, Commander of the Seraphim ...**Sacred Code 82438. To those who request it, an angel from my army will be assigned, a being related to their personalities, their functions: it will clear the way for them, so that they can advance without so many obstacles. It will help you heal any evil, and it will strongly push you toward your goals, including that of feeling close to God. It will strengthen intuition, unlock creativity.

Supernaphim

- **Supernaphim ...**Sacred Code 618

- **Supernaphim Earax ...**Sacred Code 1821, 6631 and 2812

Ascended Masters and beings of light

- **Big events (Prepare) ...** Sacred Code 1212

- **Ascended Masters (to aspire to become one with them) ...**Sacred Code 421

- **Beings of light...**Sacred Code 554. To let go and let it flow, cancel the resistances and the brakes that prevent us from receiving messages.

- **Beings of Light (telepathic contact) ...**Sacred Code 1000

- **Adama ...**Sacred Code 1576

- **Aeracura (Earth Deity) ...** Sacred Code 191919

- **Agleen ...**Sacred Code 40. A loving messenger from THE SOURCE, the one who helps you listen to the wise voices of your ancestors.

- **Alexa ...**Sacred Code 344

- **White Eagle...**Sacred Code 610

- **Andel (connect with his energy)...**Sacred Code 447

- **Telos Advisor...**Sacred Code 456. Recommended by Master Adama. It's amazing how quickly this advisor responds when we've visited. The next day he reveals to us all that he taught us in Telos during the night.

- **Babaji and Mataji Ashram...**Sacred Code 883. Whoever uses this Number will be instructed by Ba-baji and I, who will take him there while I sleep.

- **Athena...**Sacred Code 515

- **Babaji...**Sacred Code 225 and 927

- **Babaji 19...**The scope of this Number is extraordinary. The 19th attracts the Father like a magnet Celestial, to the Elohim Calm and Peaceful, to the Master Merlin, to Saint Expedito, to his beloved disincarnate Beloved Ones, and it is the key Number to invoke when they go through difficult and desperate situations.

- **Blana ...**Sacred Code 337755. Through this number, your bitterness will be healed, your victory will be assured, and your tears will be wiped away.

- **Buddha...**Sacred Code 110

- **Chico Xavier (Medium)...**Sacred Code 167

- **Solar Codes...**Sacred Code 033, 88, 559, 22000,

and 567. Intended to favorably influence the lives and needs of those who invoke them.

- **Voces de La Galaxia Collective...**Sacred Code 2680

- **Connect with the Sun...**Sacred Code 444. It will allow you to receive beneficial energies from the Astro King. They have tried to make you believe that the sun is dangerous. The sun is actually the one who warms them up and loves them. Do not fear him. It's a good friend.

- **Winged collective consciousness of nine...** Sacred Code 33377. Those of us who lovingly await your requests for help.

- **Heart of Planet Oasibeth ...**Sacred Code 71292538. They will achieve their objectives, whoever immerses himself in this vibration will enjoy special help.

- **Sacred Heart (To activate) ...** Sacred Code 123

- **Golden Cross of Oasibeth (receive the benefits) ...**Sacred Code 7733

- **Daikini Cristina ...**Sacred Code 568. I am Cristina, the one who shows you the way to the Mystical Kingdom of Shambala. We have the power of manifestation and we will accelerate it for those who invoke us.

- **White dolphins...**Sacred Code 159. We represent freedom, speed, intuition, friendship, communica- tion, wisdom, and the solution to many of your problems. Whoever invokes us will experience our beneficial vibration.

- **Of you...**Sacred Code 14. The Earth Healing Angel

- **God of gold...**Sacred Code 101. He is a servant of the Light and offers those who serve the Light an abundant supply of everything they need.

- **God of nature...**Sacred Code 98. This being governs the forces of Nature. He is a servant of the Light and offers to those who serve the Light the abundant supply of everything you need.

- **Goddess Lakshmi ...**Sacred Code 2918. The Goddess of wealth and beauty. It is believed that all those who adore her know immediate happiness.

- **God of the Violet Flame ...**Sacred Code 4973

- **Goddess of Violet Flame** ...Sacred Code 771

- **Goddess Maat (Egypt)** ...Sacred Code 225. Maat loves the right people, and takes care of them as if they were her children. The main quality of Maat is Justice. We can go to her to make this attribute shine in our favor. If any of you have any pending legal issues, turn to Maat to make transparency present. This Goddess offers great protection to decent people and delivers them from delusions and bad energies. It is of great helpto solve chaotic situations.

- **Goddess of the Seas**...Sacred Code 7521

- **Goddess Venus**...Sacred Code 87

- **Dr. José Gregorio Hernández**...Sacred Code 694. Ascended Master belongs to the Green Ray.

- **Doctor Lorphan**...Sacred Code 729, 28700, 654, 901, 733 and 1563. Galactic Healer. Whoever wants to visit his Etheric Retreat will be healed by him and his team of healers. His specialty is removing darts, bullets, and etheric arrows that are thrown by psychic vampires and other negative entities.

- **Dwal Khul**...Sacred Code 5701 and 3720

- **Lunar Sphere Heavenly Army**...Sacred Code

986. You will receive abundant graces, including liberation from karmic bondage and oppression. In addition, I will saturate them with my joyful and hopeful energy, so that they advance towards their goals. They are Gabriel, Anixiel, Atheniel, Amnediel, Amnixiel, Azariel, Abrinael, Ardifiel, Abdizuel, At-liel, Amutiel, Adriel, Azeruel, Barbiel, Bethnael, Di-rachiel, Enediel, Ergeldiel, Egibiel, Geniel, Geliel, Jazeriel, Kyriel, Neciel, Requiel, Sxheliel, tagriel, Ebvap, Ebvep, Enchede, Emtircheyud,

Emrudue, Emkebpe, Ezhesekis, Eneye, Emzhebyb, Embative, Amzhere, Emnymar, Ezhobar, Emcheva, Emnepe, Echotasa, Etamrezh, Emhom, Emzhit, Litezheviche, Emzhabetskiy, Ezhevich, Emzhabetskiye, and Lavemezhu.

- **El Morya...**Sacred Code 522. He is a great defender in case of psychic attacks. His great Decree is THE LIGHT OF GOD NEVER FAILS.

- **Sirius Diamond Energy...**Sacred Code 48815. Make this vibration conscious by decreeing: I am the Diamond Energy of Sirius, manifesting now in my life and affairs.

- **Erimihala...**Sacred Code 41. I am the one who reveals to you the secrets of the Invisible World.

  I am the healer of your subconscious mind. Say my name as a motto chant throughout the day.

This will allow them to feel my presence so clearly that their confidence will be reborn, and they will begin to make wise choices.

- **Esther (Star) Old Testament ...**Sacred Code 430. You can ask for protection against the Entities that the Master Jesus called "evil spirits."

- **Secret star of love ...**Sacred Code 51826. Through Alsemiyat and the use of this code, you will receive the Rays of this star. This will be of great benefit to you, as you will be guided by Your Inner Christ and will make your wishes come true
- **Faustina Kowalska...**Sacred Code 421

- **Platinum Flame of Master Saint Germain...** Sacred Code 464

- **Solar Violet Flame of the 5th Dimension...** Sacred Code 708

- **Forceti...**Sacred Code 1579. It is a Ce-lestial lawyer who can be called in legal matters and to resolve conflicts. Like Green Tara, and the Planetary Geboy Betor, respond immediately.

- **Ganesha...**Sacred Code 46429

- **Governors of Oasibeth...**Sacred Code 25600

- **Warriors of the Phoenix Nebula...**Sacred Code 444, 97, 114 These beings give many signs that the awakened one will see without difficulty.

- **Oasibeth Portal Guardian...** Sacred Code 442. Whoever wants to be the guardian of the portal of Oasibeth, Make frequent use of this code. This code and the 147-62 that was revealed to you by

  Merlin, will attract like a magnet towards you, the divine favors. Being the guardian of this portal is an honor, as Oasibeth will save many from ruin.

  Great thanks will be granted to those who spread the existence of this golden planet invisible to the eyes of third density. Oasibeth is located very close to the Sirian star system, and is known on the sidereal worlds as the planet of mercy.

- **Hilarion...**Sacred Code 2631

- **Horus...**Sacred Code 3671. Who wants to see better in every way, turn to me. Visualize a small image of me, in the space between your eyebrows, and I will help you open your third eye. I offer prompt and visible help, both to men and women, who want to heal their relationship with their mothers. This aspect is vital, since the relationship with the mother greatly influences their passage through the land. If you did not feel loved and welcomed by it, the world will seem somewhat uncomfortable and strange. Don't waste your time or steal it by cultivating unworthy relationships with people. I am Horus, the son of Isis, the goddess of peace.

- **Call**...Sacred Code 546. An ancient traveler from the sidereal worlds, in the service of the powerful Angel Kiliosa.

- **Call yamashi**...Sacred Code 28. I come from Ageón. I am the Commander of Squad 28 of The Consciousnesses of Light that you call "Or-bes". We can favorably alter the vibrations of the venues for your own convenience. Every time you have an important meeting or carry out some activity that produces tension, call me, and I will be there in fractions of a second to put the circumstances in your favor.

- **Iramú**...Sacred Code 584. I am at the service of the Planetary Genius Aratron, I am female. Think of any diligence that you have to do or something that you would like to achieve.

- **Isama Kamura (Ageon)**...Sacred Code 61263

- **Ishao Kamata**...Sacred Code 688 and 604. I am the one who reveals the secrets of The Numbers,

The Colors, and The Words.

- **Isis...**Sacred Code 717

- **Ixapasemil...**Sacred Code 2113. One of the Guardians of the Eight Moons, the one who perches on the agitated sea of the mind until it becomes serene and calm.

- **John the Baptist...**Sacred Code 538

- **Jua The Egyptian...**Sacred Code 836

- **Joan of Arc...**Sacred Code 2021

- **Karmic Board...**Sacred Code 481 and 262. Members: kwan yin, Portia, Alexa, Pallas Athena, Lady Nada, Mother Mary, Elohim sight "the eye all watchful 'of god, Shri lean, lord Saithrhu.

• **Kuan Kung (one of the most important De- ities in China)...**Sacred Code 708. This Warrior,bearer of the greatest attributes, is a great protector and attracts prosperity. You can grant manyfavors to whoever calls you or has your image athome, office, farm, or business.

- **Kwan Yin (mother of mercy)...**Sacred Code 286

- **The Triune Flame...**Sacred Code 4972

- **Lady Rowena...**Sacred Code 82137

- **Lady Venus...**Sacred Code 715. The one that teaches them true love, respect, and honesty.

- **Lahiri Mahasaya...**Sacred Code 244

- **Lanto...**Sacred Code 111

- **Legrashogua...**Sacred Code 1596. He is one of the teachers of Jesus the Christ, who initiated him into the wisdom of the arcana. Go to him, and ask him to pass on his knowledge to you. It is an entity of the phoenix nebula. It helps to eliminate "symptoms" that negative entities cause, such as illnesses, discomforts, and hopeless situations, respiratory problems, intense colds, pain, fears, guilt, psychological aggressions, sexual dysfunctions.

- **Violet Flame...**Sacred Code 801. Recommended
- **Violet Flame (Be more aware of her) ...**Sacred Code 124. If you use it, you will see how this Flame will shine in you with more intensity than ever, and you will no longer want to separate from it.

- **Violet Flame of the Great Silence ...** Sacred Code 347

- **Violet Flame of the Great Central Sun ...**Sacred Code 1500

- **Violet flame of the thousand suns ...** Sacred Code 860907. The Violet Flame pulses through our Heart Flames and blazes in, through and around all inharmonious actions, all lower human consciousness and all obstructions of the Light that any person, place, conditions. -tion, or has placed him on the path of perfection of Life. Instantly, the Violet Flame Transmutes this discordant energy cause, core, effect, record, and memory back to its original perfection.

- **Silver violet flame (For everything) ...**Sacred Code 524

- **The Warriors of the Sun ...**Sacred Code 525. They will increase your faith in such a way that it will magnetize your dreams in a way that you never imagined.
- **The Healers of the Sun ...**Sacred Code 12543. We are the ones who always listen to your prayers.

- **Lord (Lord) Dattatreya ...**Sacred Code 591.

I am, the incarnation of The Holy Trinity Brah-ma, Vishnu, and Shiva, the one who promptly answers the prayers of the poor and afflicted. Anyone not satisfied with their current situation, turn to me.

Whoever lacks prosperity will receive it from me. Whoever believes that he is the object of curses, I will deliver him. Whoever does not have health, through me will obtain it. Who is afraid, come to me. Who in his field needs rain, I will send it to him. Whoever wants to be free from the wheel of incarnations, will obtain this grace from me.

- **The 7 Rays ...**Sacred Code 2620 and 929

- **Akasha White Light ...**Sacred Code 1550

- **Master Akkao Tami ...**Sacred Code 2870

- **Teacher Amira Sasaki ...**Sacred Code 2871. Their specialty is Telepsychia or Distance Influence.

- **Master Afra ...**Sacred Code 1613

- **Divine Mother (Mesime Ship)** ...Sacred Code 717

- **Mother Sekhmet** ...Sacred Code 11129. The protector. Every time you are going to face those situations that you call difficult, unpleasant, tedious or that instill fear, call me, for me they are challenges and I like them. I'll be there to enlighten you. Print my image and keep it close, I can endow it with power.

- **Maharishi M. Yogi** ...Sacred Code 425

- **Black Manjushri** ...Sacred Code 2431

- **Blue Mantle of Grace** ...Sacred Code 174

- **Marcoam** ...Sacred Code 516. One of my missions is to open the doors of psycho-logical prisons, in which those souls who suffered sexual abuse in their childhood are captive. I am the help for these souls. I carry out this work in the company of Doctor Lorphan, an eminent galactic healer. Another of my missions is to dismantle hosts of negative entities that threaten their well-being in the places they frequent and inhabit.

- **Marta Ruth** ...Sacred Code 68115. Carrier of the Syrian diamond energy. Ask to be under his protection and receive his blessing.

- **Mataji** ...Sacred Code 799 and 294 divine complement of Babaji

- **Melina (divine complement of White Eagle)** ...Sacred Code 914

- **Melkizadek** ...Sacred Code 11614. In case of psychic attacks

- **Marline**...Sacred Code 477965. To connect and thus attract our desires, I ask that the magician in me awaken

- **Mornah Simeona** ...Sacred Code 1570

- **White Buffalo Woman** ...Sacred Code 3

- **Murugan** ... Sacred Code 52574. I can help you in legal matters, business. To improve your health. I protect you from malicious people, enemies, and negative entities. They can also Summon me when they do a business (purchase, sale, exchange).

- **Purple Sea Ship**...Sacred Code 10028. Where Kwan Yin will be waiting for you with infinite love.

- **Neida and Awara**...Sacred Codes 363 and 560 respectively. Entities of Light in charge of sending the VIOLET FLAME to Earth.

- **Nirmala Sundari**...Sacred Codes 504
- **Osiris**...Sacred Code 2120

- **Ossok...**Sacred Code 808. Those who want to work on the liberation of the Eighth Ray can call on this being.

- **Paul the Venetian...**Sacred Code 232

- **Padmasambhava...**Sacred Code 2690

- **Padre Pio...**Sacred Code 4447

  - **To attract the mercy of the Bodhisat-tvas...** Sacred Code 811

- **To attract blessings from the Magi...**Sacred Code 554

- **Parvati...**Sacred Code 4990

- **Pyramid of Power (5 Dimension), Archangel Michael...**Sacred Code 1515

- **Ageón Portal (Open)...**Sacred Code 1929216. The Ascended Master Merlin offers us this code that will repair all the damage that has been done to them.

- **Portal in Andromeda...**Sacred Code 615

- **Portal in the Pleiades...**Sacred Code 219

- **Oasibeth Portal (open)...**Sacred Code 147-62

- **Portal of the Golden Feather...**Sacred Code 1216. When you open it, they will go into action and on our behalf, LOS ANGELES ACCELERATORS. These Beings of Light as the word says, "Accelerate",speed things up so that we can achieve our goals in the shortest time possible.

- **Gray Feather...**Sacred Code 68025. Daughter of the Ascended Master White Eagle and Melina if you want to see miracles, call this Family of Light

- **Prophets Moses...**Sacred Code 85012

- **Prophets Elijah...**Sacred Code 52071

- **Ra...**Sacred Code 16

- **Ramtha...**Sacred Code 659

- **Receive energy from Mount Shasta...**Code 523

- **Receiving gifts from Ishao Kamata...**Code Sacred Code 1615. She is a Being of extraordinary beauty, and a wonderful confidant.

- **Receive gifts from John the Elder...**Sacred Code for: 181. He is very close to Mother Mary and is the possessor of great wisdom.

- **King Solomon...**Sacred Code 344 Highest level soul, you can ask him for wisdom and help in cases that seem impossible. Free from fear and ignorance. Teaches to solve difficult situations.

- **Rosa Mystica (Mysterious Rose)...** Sacred Code 6843. Our heavenly nurse.

- **Ruth of Andromeda (Tune in with her energy)...**Sacred Code 5600. I will wipe the tears from their eyes and comfort their souls. I am a faithful messenger of Mother Mary for this hour.

- **Sai Baba...**Sacred Code 8888, 7194, 559, and 150. The one who knows your needs, even before they ask me for them. The 559 is an ascension accelerator, and the 150 is to help those who so desire, to contact nature.

- **Saint Germain...**Sacred Code 523

- **Saint Germain (Special Protection)...**Sacred Code 4444444

- **Sanat Kumara (make contact)...**Sacred Code 449

- **Time Lords...**Sacred Code 365365

- **Time Lords...**Sacred Code 55555

- **Lord Omri-Tas (Governor of the Violet Planet)**...Sacred Code 679. It grants great blessings to those who work with La llama Viole-ta.

- **Serapis Bey** ...Sacred Code 68120

- **Simon** ...Sacred Code 68116. I am Simon a Tutelary Spirit, a lamp that illuminates your steps.

- **Simon Bolivar**...Sacred Code 155. This being of light possesses a very high vibration.

- **Shiddarta (connection)** ...Sacred Code 52637

- **Shiva** ...Sacred Code 351. I am in charge of ensuring respect for creation. I am the god of the outcast and my compassion is extraordinary. I am the one who reveals the most hidden truths, the one who has power over nature and the elements.

- **Sirius Sun (Blue Ray)** ...Sacred Code 021

- **Soo Shee**...Sacred Code 26600. I am the one who leads you to live in the serene regions of harmonious thought, and offers you the treasure of compassion.

- **Mr. Surya**...Sacred Code 64

- **White Tara**...Sacred Code 518. It is an enlightened feminine being whose function is to impart a long life, wisdom and good fortune. If we trust it with faith, it will protect us from contagious diseases, fire hazards, and other disasters. It is said that sentient beings receive the blessings of Tara as swiftly as the movement of the wind since she is the manifestation of the wind element of all Buddhas.

- **Green Tara...**Sacred Code 517 and 659. I am green tara, the star that frees from dangers, the one that answers their prayers instantly, and takes action to favor them. She represents the compassion of all Buddhas, she is very quick in her action.

- **Thot...**Sacred Code 711

- **Karmic Court...**Sacred Code 3157. General Code

- **Vajrapani...**Sacred Code 1612

- **Silent Nightstand...**Sacred Code 594

- **Yogi Ramacharaca...**Sacred Code 22233

- **The 3 wise men...**Sacred Code 554

- **Dr. Alexis Carrel ...**Sacred Code 929. Notable physician and writer, author of the phrase "Dowsing can save the world." Anyone who wants to make accurate readings with the pendulum, and be successful in this field, Alexis Carrel is the best Mentor they can have.

- **Dr. David Stone ...**Sacred Code 711

- **Dr. Francisco Antonio Mesmer ...** Sacred Code 58179. He was born in 1733. He is considered the precursor of Hypnotism. He argued that the stars, the sun, and the moon exert an influence on the human organism through an energy that he called animal magnetism. It can be said that Mesmer was the first of the Modern Psychologists and the first Therapist. His cures were extraordinary. In 1815, he died in a German Duchy of Swabia.

- **Dr. Erich Fromm ...**Sacred Code 72515. (While he was incarnated as well as a noble writer, he was an expert in the field of psychoanalysis. If any of you want to learn to know yourself and have the help of a great therapist, Erich Fromm will advise you in dreams , and will help you solve your own problems. It will also put you in contact with honest therapists and therapists, from which you can learn very useful things. For the sake of brevity, I do not elaborate on the explanation, so whoever wants to know more about these Beings of Light, Google or do some research on their own.)

- **Dr. Joseph Murphy ...**Sacred Code 55533. (He was an authority in the field of the mind, and wrote more than 30 books. He was a scholar. Whoever wants to develop his potential to the maximum and live a successful life, will achieve it with the help of this great Counselor).

- **Dr. Paul Jagot ...**Sacred Code 73. (1889-1962). He was born and lived in Paris. His Literary Work has had an influence all over the world. His wonderful books have healed and helped thousands of Souls. He was an expert in The Fields of Hypnosis, Psychology, Astrology, Magnetism, Suggestion, Occult Sciences, Magic, and all areas related to self-control and self-improvement. If any of you, for example, work with Hypnosis, Paul Jagot will be a wonderful Mentor. It can teach you to apply

hypnosis successfully and honestly, as he did while on earth. He can undoubtedly be the best of the Masters and he will receive signs and enlightenment from this great man.

- **Dr. William Parker ...**Sacred Code 380. This Code will free whoever uses it, from fear, guilt, feelings of inferiority, and hatred.

- **Luca Paccioli ...**Sacred Code 28

- **Neville Goddard ...**Sacred Code 61571. (1905-1972), He was a notable Psychic Researcher, Lecturer and Writer. You can find a lot of material about him on Google and YouTube. His knowledge of applied metaphysics can be used in daily life with success. For me, the greatest teaching that this Spiritual Giant can offer us is everything related to imagination. Neville can help you visualize successfully. He was a Master on this subject. Most people have their visualization power blocked, making it difficult for them to construct mental images. Rest assured that if you work with Neville, he will help you and listen to you. Finally I leave you a phrase from him: "I know my time is short - I finished the work I came to do and now I am ready to go. I know that I will not return to this three-dimensional world again, but I have kept my promise.

- **Guru Gobinda ...**Sacred Code 11577. (1666-1708). He was a warrior of sublime compassion, he abolished slavery in India. He was a heroic leader who overcame many obstacles. This Mentor helps by granting strength, favors those who like to write, he was a scholar. His Mantras are excellent and whoever asks for his help will eliminate the negativity by means of his Cosmic Sword. Give signals to whoever calls you.

- **Pythagoras...**Sacred Code 1354. I want to be the Master of whoever calls me. I am a very Spiritual entity, and I have the honor to be part of the Spiritual Mentor Program. I love teaching, and I love Numbers, so I welcome those who want to be my students. I am Pythagoras, the one who invites you to surrender to your divine missions without doubts, and right now.

- **Albert Einstein...**Sacred Code 25630

- **Bruce Lee...**Sacred Code 487. The reason why I chose to assist the earth is the unbelief of most people, If the ingredient of faith is absent, No dream is fulfilled, and what is more regrettable , one goes through life in a mediocre way and without using the talents of the soul. This light that I offer will reach those who believe in the magic and love of the universe. Nothing is accidental in the fabric of existence, and the In-finite smiles at those who believe the impossible.

- **Dr. Eduard Bach (Flower Essences) ...**Sacred Code 21700

- **Dr. Mikao Usui ...**Sacred Code 1515

- **Conny Mendez ...**Sacred Code 1229

- **Guru Padmashambava ...**Sacred Code 2690

- **Lao Tse...**Sacred Code 62115. An old friend who speaks to you in silence.

- **Nichiren Daishonin ...**Sacred Code 113

To request a spiritual mentor

- **Ask for a mentor in the area of health...**Sacred Code 27915

  - **Ask for a mentor in the area of nutrition and feeding ...**Sacred Code 62013

- **Ask for a mentor in the work area...**Sacred Code 82820

- **Ask for a mentor in the area of friendships...**Sacred Code 52515

- **Ask for a mentor in the Psychic area...**Sacred Code 52119

  - **Ask for a mentor in the business area...** Sacred Code 72911

Stellar beings

- **Asthar...**Sacred Code 1164

- **Athor...**Sacred Code 25793. Commander of the Pleiadian interstellar fleet in the service of Tera.

- **Commander Amún...**Sacred Code 771

- **Commander Julian of Arcturus...**Sacred Code 15415

- **Connection with Alsemiyat...**Sacred Code72599. Commander of the Fire Warriors.

- **Cristina of Andromeda ...**Sacred Code 699, 101 and 313

- **Ellionen ...**Sacred Code 1613

- **Ixapasemil...**Sacred Code 2113

- **Andromeda Light...**Sacred Code 101 and 5600

- **Marcoam...**Sacred Code 516

- **Mysterious world...**Sacred Code 280

- **Nave Leen (Commanders Saer and Ayat)...** Sacred Code 1919. Whoever calls us can be sure that we will eliminate any aggression on the part of those beings who are not respecting the freedom to which you are entitled.

- **Mothership Anais...**Sacred Code 928

- **Ship Tuly...**Sacred Code 526

- **Phoenix Bird Nebula...**Sacred Code 444, 97, 114

- **Cosmic name...**Sacred Code 76129. It is the one that identifies you in the Universe. This Name can be revealed just like our Agesta Channel does. The being that you know as José Gabriel here on earth, is identified as Agesta in other Dimensions.

- **Secret Name.** It is a sound that your innermost being will reveal to you, and that in turn, you will not reveal to anyone, that is why it is called "secret". To have access to these treasures, you can call us. Before using it you can say something like this: Powers of the angelic realm of the thirteenth dimension, Lighten our ascension process and allow us to experience your guidance and protection here and now.

- **Earthly name ...**the one they chose to incarnate. Your names have a particular vibration that will clear your inner channels so that your soul can speak to you. By repeating the name daily (always 45 times, like the codes) they will connect to mother earth, and will attract the life they deserve.

- **Ruth of Andromeda ...**Sacred Code 5600

- **Sirius Salusa ...**Sacred Code 177

- **Shasha member of La Nave Tuly ...**Sacred Code 823

- **Sheila from Sirius ...**Sacred Code 55124

The Elohim

- **Elohim Tranquility** ...Sacred Code 129. This great Being grants that inner peace so necessary today.

- **Elohim Pacifica** ...Sacred Code 1139. Divine complement of elohim tranquility.

- **Elohim Vista** ...Sacred Code 52911 and 280. The All Watchful Eye "of God.

- **Elohim Arcturus** ...Sacred Code 522. "I AM" the Elohim of INVOCATION and RHYTHM, who bringsyou and all life, through the use of the Violet Fire, THE INFINITE LIBERATION - when they want it enough! "I AM" That Who responds to the call of the heartbeat of any individual when that heart, deeply and sincerely, from within itself, wishes to liberate the life that has become a bondage by giv-ing it LIBERATION from disease, lack, fear and the limitation of all kinds and descriptions.

- **Orion and Angelica**...Sacred Code 25600 and 12500 respectively

- **Cassiopeia and Minerva**...Sacred Codes 318 and 411 respectively

- **Hercules and Amazonia**...Sacred Code 521

and 632 respectively

- **Glass...**Sacred Code 531. Divine complement of elohim Vista

- **Clarity (Purity) and Astrea ...**Sacred Code 724 and 323 respectively

- **Arcthurus and Diana ...**Sacred Code 522 and 529 respectively

Planetary geniuses

- **Monday Planetary Genius Phul...**Sacred Code 1004. Governs the affairs of the Moon. Heals dropsy, and grants undines that help us in a visible way. Angel of purity. Invoked for Learning, Mentalization, Feminine, and Prophecy. White color.

- **Tuesday Planetary Genius Phaleg...**Sacred Code 62987. Governs the affairs of Mars. Gives peace, and helps to manage and control the Ego. Angel of simplicity. It is invoked for Victories. Red color.

- **Wednesday Planetary Genius Ophiel...**Sacred Code 1008. Governs the affairs of Mercury. Teaches all the Arts, and grants Family Spirits. Angel of Activity. It is invoked for Oratory and loquacity. Color blue.

- **Thursday Planetary Genius Bethor...**Sacred Code 1010. Governs the affairs of Ju-piter. It grants Sylphs of Light that give us correct answers. Provides miracle drugs. Family spirits can be requested for the needs we have. Angel of Moderation. It is invoked for Intercessor of orators and conductors of great masses. Violet Color.

- **Friday Planetary Genius Hagith...**Sacred Code 1012. Governs the affairs of Venus. It grants beauty and good things. He also gives Family Spirits so that we can entrust them with missions specific. Angel of Nobility. It is invoked for Love in all its facets. Green color.

- **Saturday Aratron Planetary Genius...**Sacred Code 1014. Governs the Affairs of Saturn. Teaches magic, physics, and alchemy. Gives us

  Familiar spirits for specific matters. He also grants us the friendship of The Pygmies of Light. Angel of Generosity, It is invoked to separate enemies and guard against setbacks. Color Brown or Black. This is one of the Geniuses who helped Aladdin. The story of Aladdin is real.

- **Planetary Genius Sunday Och...**Sacred Code 1016. It governs the affairs of the Sun. It teaches medicine, wisdom, and gives money. He has at his service 36,536 Spirits, and he sends them according to the needs of each one. Angel of Serenity. It is invoked for Abundance and Honor. Yellow or Gold Color.

Elementals of nature

- **Earth element...** Sacred Code 664 The members of this Element can help us to connect with the Earth, and to acquire material goods and abundance. This is not a fantasy, as they are the guardians of the treasures. We can ask them to teach us the art of discipline, order, and persistence.

- **Air Element...**Numerical Sacred Code 1690. We can ask its members for faith and hope, protection, and consolation in pain.

- **Water element...**Sacred Code 1810. The Beings of this Element if we request them, will improve our intuition, and our ability to visualize. They also make us aware of our power.

- **Fire element...**Sacred Code 2140. They can help us develop daring and be free. They love it when you have a lit candle in your home.

- **Contact with Gnome...**Sacred Code 55

- **Contact with Fairies...**Sacred Code 5510

- **Contact with Sirens...**Sacred Code 772

- **Contact with Salamanders...**Sacred Code 271

- **Genius PHUL (Monday)...**Sacred Code 1004. Itgrants ONDINAS that help us in a visible way.

- **Salamanders...**Sacred Code 2715

- **Genius BETHOR (Thursday)...**Sacred Code 1010. It grants SILFOS of Light that give us cor-rect answers.

- **The Kingdom of the Fairies wants to be present through BABA and JULIA, whomthey can call with the...**Sacred Code 515 and 2515 respectively.

- **Sybila a fairy from The Divine Source...** Sacred Code 3330. Knows many secrets.

- **Fairies of Oasibeth...**Sacred Code 33399. "We want to be friends with the men and women who have awakened, we are fun and we are present in nature and in the countryside. We are protecting the environment and all natural resources we want to meet you in parks, meadows, and trees.

  We are very healing and happy we can remove the fear from your souls, come out to meet us with-out delay and we will manifest our magic to you.

We want to heal Mother Earth BELIEVE even if they cannot see us at first, if they believe in us, theygive us strength and we will reveal their talents to them. We know the hearts of men and we can makethem happier by helping them to produce mira- cles and heal and improve their lives. So look for the natural areas and start conversations with us.

If you ask for help, it will never be denied and youwill have the life you always dreamed of. "

- **Fairy Paradise...**Sacred Code 580

- **Communication with the Kingdom of Sirens...**Sacred Code 27620

Fantastic Beings

- **Kingdom of unicorns ...**Sacred Code 14147

- **Pegasi ...**Sacred Code 003

Made in the USA
Las Vegas, NV
14 April 2024

88672726R00125